Programme for International Student Assessment

The PISA 2003 Assessment Framework –

Mathematics,
Reading,
Science and
Problem Solving
Knowledge and Skills

OECD
ORGANISATION FOR ECONOMIC CO-OPERATION AND DEVELOPMENT

ORGANISATION FOR ECONOMIC CO-OPERATION AND DEVELOPMENT

Pursuant to Article 1 of the Convention signed in Paris on 14th December 1960, and which came into force on 30th September 1961, the Organisation for Economic Co-operation and Development (OECD) shall promote policies designed:

- to achieve the highest sustainable economic growth and employment and a rising standard of living in member countries, while maintaining financial stability, and thus to contribute to the development of the world economy;

- to contribute to sound economic expansion in member as well as non-member countries in the process of economic development; and

- to contribute to the expansion of world trade on a multilateral, non-discriminatory basis in accordance with international obligations.

The original member countries of the OECD are Austria, Belgium, Canada, Denmark, France, Germany, Greece, Iceland, Ireland, Italy, Luxembourg, the Netherlands, Norway, Portugal, Spain, Sweden, Switzerland, Turkey, the United Kingdom and the United States. The following countries became members subsequently through accession at the dates indicated hereafter: Japan (28th April 1964), Finland (28th January 1969), Australia (7th June 1971), New Zealand (29th May 1973), Mexico (18th May 1994), the Czech Republic (21st December 1995), Hungary (7th May 1996), Poland (22nd November 1996), Korea (12th December 1996) and the Slovak Republic (14th December 2000). The Commission of the European Communities takes part in the work of the OECD (Article 13 of the OECD Convention).

Publié en français sous le titre :

Cadre d'évaluation de PISA 2003
Connaissances et compétences en mathématiques, lecture, science et résolution de problèmes

Table of contents

Foreword

The OECD Programme for International Student Assessment (PISA), created in 1997, represents a commitment by the governments of OECD Member countries to monitor the outcomes of education systems in terms of student achievement, within a common international framework. OECD/PISA is, above all, a collaborative effort, bringing together scientific expertise from the participating countries and steered jointly by their governments on the basis of shared, policy-driven interests. Participating countries take responsibility for the project at the policy level. Experts from participating countries also serve on working groups that are charged with linking the OECD/PISA policy objectives with the best available substantive and technical expertise in the field of internationally comparative assessment. Through participating in these expert groups, countries ensure that the OECD/PISA assessment instruments are internationally valid and take into account the cultural and curricular context of OECD Member countries; have strong measurement properties; and, place an emphasis on authenticity and educational validity.

PISA 2003 represents a continuation of the data strategy adopted in 1997 by OECD countries and the assessed domains build on those used in PISA 2000. However, while the emphasis in PISA 2000 was on the assessment of reading literacy, the focus of PISA 2003 is now on mathematical literacy, defined as the capacity of students to identify, understand and engage in mathematics and to make well-founded judgements about the role that mathematics plays in life. In addition, an assessment of problem-solving skills has been integrated as a new element into PISA, defined as the ability of students to use cognitive processes to solve real cross-disciplinary problems where the solution path is not obvious.

This publication presents the guiding principles of the PISA 2003 assessment, described in terms of the content that students need to acquire, the processes that need to be performed, and the contexts in which knowledge and skills are applied. It also illustrates the assessment domains with a range of sample tasks. These have been developed by expert panels under the direction of Raymond Adams, Barry McCrae, Ross Turner and Margaret Wu of the Australian Council for Educational Research (ACER). The mathematics panel was chaired by Jan de Lange of the University of Utrecht in the Netherlands, the reading expert panel was chaired by Irwin Kirsch of the Educational Testing Service in the United States, the science expert panel was chaired by Wynne Harlen from the United Kingdom, and the problem solving panel was chaired by John Dossey of Illinois State University from the United States. The members of the expert groups are listed in the Appendix of this publication. The frameworks have also been reviewed by expert panels in each of the participating countries.

This publication was prepared by the OECD Directorate for Education, under the responsibility of Andreas Schleicher and Claudia Tamassia. This report is published on the responsibility of the Secretary-General of the OECD. ⌋

Introduction to the OECD/PISA 2003 Assessment

OVERVIEW

The OECD Programme for International Student Assessment (PISA) is a collaborative effort on the part of the Member countries of the OECD to measure how well students at age 15, and therefore approaching the end of compulsory schooling, are prepared to meet the challenges of today's societies. The OECD/PISA assessment takes a broad approach to assessing knowledge and skills that reflect the current changes in curricula, moving beyond the school based approach towards the use of knowledge in everyday tasks and challenges. These skills reflect the ability of students to continue learning throughout their lives by applying what they learn in school to non-school environments, evaluating their choices and making decisions. The assessment, jointly steered by the participating governments, brings together the policy interest of countries with scientific expertise at the national and international levels.

OECD/PISA combines the assessment of domain-specific areas such as reading, mathematical and scientific literacy with important cross-curricular areas, also a priority among OECD countries. These areas are covered through an assessment of self-regulated learning and information technologies, complemented in 2003 by an assessment of problem solving skills. The outcomes are then associated with contextual information on students, families and institutions collected through the questionnaires. OECD/PISA is based on: *i)* strong quality assurance mechanisms for translation, sampling and data collection; *ii)* measures to achieve cultural and linguistic breadth in the assessment materials, particularly through countries' participation in the development and revision processes and the cultural review panels; and *iii)* the latest methodology for data analysis. The combination of these measures produces high quality instruments and outcomes with superior levels of validity and reliability to improve the understanding of education systems and students' characteristics.

OECD/PISA is based on a dynamic model of lifelong learning in which new knowledge and skills necessary for successful adaptation to a changing world are continuously acquired throughout life. OECD/PISA focuses on things that 15-year-olds will need in the future and seeks to assess what they can do with what they have learned. The assessment is informed – but not constrained – by the common denominator of national curricula. Thus, while OECD/PISA does assess students' knowledge, it also examines their ability to reflect, and to apply their knowledge and experience to real-world issues. For example, in order to understand and evaluate scientific advice on food safety, an adult would need not only to know some basic facts about the composition of nutrients, but also to be able to apply that information. The term "literacy" is used to encapsulate this broader conception of knowledge and skills.

OECD/PISA was designed to collect information promptly and efficiently through three-yearly cycles. It presents data on the reading, mathematical and scientific literacy of students, schools and countries, provides insights into the factors that influence the development of the skills at home and at school, and examines how these factors interact and what the implications are for policy development.

This publication presents the conceptual framework underlying the PISA 2003 assessments: the framework for the assessment of reading and scientific literacy from PISA 2000, an expanded framework for the in-depth assessment of mathematical literacy, as well as the framework for the new assessment of problem solving as a cross-curricular competency. Within each domain, the framework defines the content that students need to acquire, the processes that need to be performed and the contexts in which knowledge and skills are applied. Finally, it illustrates the domains and their aspects with sample tasks.

BASIC FEATURES OF PISA 2003

PISA 2003 is the second cycle of a data strategy defined in 1997 by participating countries. The publication *Measuring Student Knowledge and Skills – A New Framework for Assessment* (OECD, 1999) presented the conceptual framework underlying the first cycle, known as PISA 2000. The results from that first cycle, presented in December 2001 in the publication *Knowledge and Skills for Life – First Results from PISA 2000* (OECD, 2001)[1], allows national policy makers to compare the performance of their education systems with those of other countries. Similar to PISA 2000, the 2003 assessment covers the domains of reading, mathematical and scientific literacy, with the major focus shifting from reading literacy towards mathematical literacy. Furthermore, the ability of students to solve problems in real-life settings is examined through an assessment of problem solving. Students also respond to a background questionnaire, and additional supporting information is gathered from the school authorities. Forty-two countries, including all 30 OECD Member countries, are taking part in the PISA 2003 assessment.

Since the aim of OECD/PISA is to assess the cumulative yield of education systems at an age where schooling is compulsory, testing will focus on 15-year-olds enrolled in both school-based and work-based educational programmes. Between 5 000 and 10 000 students from at least 150 schools will typically be tested in each country, providing a good sampling base from which to break down the results according to a range of student characteristics.

---

1. This publication is also available through the Web address *www.pisa.oecd.org.*

Box A ■ What is OECD/PISA?

A summary of key features

Basics

- An internationally standardised assessment that was jointly developed by participating countries and administered to 15-year-olds in educational programmes.

- A survey implemented in 43 countries in the first cycle (32 in 2000 and 11 in 2002) and in 42 countries in the second cycle (2003).

- Tests typically administered to between 4 500 and 10 000 students in each country.

Content

- OECD/PISA 2003 covers the domains of reading, mathematical and scientific literacy not so much in terms of mastery of the school curriculum, but in terms of important knowledge and skills needed in adult life. The examination of cross-curriculum competencies continues to be an integral part of OECD/PISA through the assessment of a new domain of problem solving.

- Emphasis is on the mastery of processes, the understanding of concepts and the ability to function in various situations within each domain.

Methods

- Paper-and-pencil tests are used, with assessments lasting a total of two hours for each student.

- Test items are a mixture of multiple-choice items and questions requiring students to construct their own responses. The items are organised in groups based on a passage setting out a real-life situation.

- A total of about seven hours of test items is covered, with different students taking different combinations of test items.

- Students answer a background questionnaire, which takes 30 minutes to complete, providing information about themselves and their homes. School principals are given a 20-minute questionnaire about their schools.

Assessment cycle

- The assessment takes place every three years: 2000, 2003 and 2006.

- Each of these cycles looks in depth at a "major" domain, to which two-thirds of testing time is devoted; the other domains provide a summary profile of skills. Major domains are reading literacy in 2000, mathematical literacy in 2003 and scientific literacy in 2006.

Outcomes

- A basic profile of knowledge and skills among 15-year-old students.

- Contextual indicators relating results to student and school characteristics.

- Trend indicators showing how results change over time.

- A valuable knowledge base for policy analysis and research.

The primary aim of the OECD/PISA assessment is to determine the extent to which young people have acquired the wider knowledge and skills in reading, mathematical and scientific literacy that they will need in adult life. The assessment of cross-curricular competencies has been made an integral part of PISA 2003 through the assessment of problem solving. The main reasons for this broadly oriented approach are as follows:

- Although specific knowledge acquisition is important in school learning, the application of that knowledge in adult life depends crucially on the acquisition of broader concepts and skills. In *mathematics*, being able to reason quantitatively and to represent relationships or dependencies is more apt than the ability to answer familiar textbook questions when it comes to deploying mathematical skills in everyday life. In *reading*, the capacity to develop interpretations of written material and to reflect on the content and qualities of text are central skills. In *science*, having specific knowledge, such as the names of plants and animals, is of less value than understanding broad topics such as energy consumption, biodiversity and human health in thinking about the issues under debate in the adult community. In *problem solving*, recognising a problem, formulating its exact nature, using this knowledge to plan a strategy for solving it, adjusting the solution to better fit the original problem, and communicating the solution to others are seen as basic skills for future learning.

- In an international setting, a focus on curriculum content would restrict attention to curriculum elements common to all or most countries. This would force many compromises and result in an assessment that was too narrow to be of value for governments wishing to learn about the strengths and innovations in the education systems of other countries.

- Certain broad, general skills are essential for students to develop. They include communication, adaptability, flexibility, problem solving and the use of information technologies. These skills are developed across the curriculum and an assessment of them requires a cross-curricular focus.

Students cannot learn in school everything they will need to know in adult life. What they must acquire is the prerequisites for successful learning in the future. Students must be able to organise and regulate their own learning, to learn independently and in groups, and to overcome difficulties in the learning process. This requires them to be aware of their own thinking processes, learning strategies and methods. Moreover, further learning will increasingly occur in situations in which people work together and are dependent on one another. To assess these aspects, an instrument seeking information on self-regulated learning was included as an optional component of the PISA 2000 assessment and as a core component in PISA 2003.

OECD/PISA is not a single cross-national assessment of the reading, mathematics and science skills of 15-year-olds. It is an on-going programme that, over the longer term, will lead to the development of a body of information for monitoring trends in the knowledge and skills of students in various countries as well as in different demographic sub-groups of each country. On each occasion, one domain will be tested in detail, taking up nearly two-thirds of the total testing time. The "major" domain was reading literacy in 2000; it will be mathematical literacy in 2003 and scientific literacy in 2006. This will provide a thorough analysis of achievement in each area every nine years and a trend analysis every three.

Similar to PISA 2000, the total time spent on the PISA 2003 tests by each student is two hours, but information is obtained on almost seven hours' worth of test items. The total set of questions is packaged into several linked testing booklets. Each booklet is taken by a sufficient number of students for appropriate estimates to be made of the achievement levels on all items by students in each country and in relevant sub-groups within a country (such as males and females, and students from different social and economic contexts). Students also spend 30 minutes answering questions for the context questionnaire.

The OECD/PISA assessment provides three main types of outcomes:

- *basic indicators* providing a baseline profile of the knowledge and skills of students;

- *contextual indicators* showing how such skills relate to important demographic, social, economic and educational variables;

- *indicators on trends* that emerge from the on-going nature of the data collection and that show changes in outcome levels and distributions, and in relationships between student-level and school-level background variables and outcomes.

Although indicators are an adequate means of drawing attention to important issues, they are not usually capable of providing answers to policy questions. OECD/PISA has therefore also developed a policy-oriented analysis plan that will go beyond the reporting of indicators.

WHAT MAKES PISA UNIQUE

OECD/PISA is not the first international comparative survey of student achievement. Others have been conducted over the past 40 years, primarily developed by the International Association for the Evaluation of Educational Achievement (IEA) and by the Education Testing Service's International Assessment of Educational Progress (IAEP). Although the quality and scope of these surveys have greatly improved over the years, they still provide only partial and sporadic information about student achievement in limited subject areas.

More importantly, these surveys have concentrated on outcomes linked directly to the curriculum and then only to those parts of the curriculum that are essentially common across the participating countries. Aspects of the curriculum unique to one country or a small number of countries have usually not been taken into account in the assessments, regardless of how significant those parts of the curriculum are for the countries involved.

OECD/PISA takes a distinctive approach in a number of important respects:

- Its *origin*. An initiative taken by governments, whose policy interests the results are addressing.

- Its *regularity*. The commitment to cover multiple assessment domains with updates every three years makes it possible for countries to monitor regularly and predictably their progress in meeting key learning objectives.

- The *age-group covered*. Assessing young people near the end of their compulsory schooling gives a useful indication of the performance of education systems. While most young people in OECD countries continue their initial education beyond the age of 15, this is normally close to the end of the initial period of basic schooling in which all young people follow a broadly common curriculum. It is useful to determine, at that stage, the extent to which they have acquired knowledge and skills that will help them in the future, including the individualised paths of further learning they may follow.

- The *knowledge and skills tested*. These are defined not primarily in terms of a common denominator of national school curricula but in terms of what skills are deemed to be essential for future life. This is the most fundamental feature of OECD/PISA. School curricula are traditionally constructed largely in terms of bodies of information and techniques to be mastered. They traditionally focus less, within curriculum areas, on the skills to be developed in each domain for use generally in adult life. They focus even less on more general competencies, developed across the curriculum, to solve problems and apply ideas and understanding to situations encountered in life. OECD/PISA does not exclude curriculum-based knowledge and understanding, but it tests for it mainly in terms of the acquisition of broad concepts and skills that allow knowledge to be applied. Further, OECD/PISA is not constrained by the common denominator of what has been specifically taught in the schools of participating countries.

This emphasis on testing in terms of mastery and broad concepts is particularly significant in light of the concern among nations to develop human capital, which the OECD defines as:

"the knowledge, skills, competencies and other attributes embodied in individuals that are relevant to personal, social and economic well-being".

Estimates of human capital have tended, at best, to be derived using proxies such as level of education completed. When the interest in human capital is extended to include attributes that permit full social and democratic participation in adult life and that equip people to become "lifelong learners", the inadequacy of these proxies becomes even clearer.

By directly testing for knowledge and skills close to the end of basic schooling, OECD/PISA examines the degree of preparedness of young people for adult life and, to some extent, the effectiveness of education systems. Its ambition is to assess achievement in relation to the underlying objectives (as defined by society) of education systems, not in relation to the teaching and learning of a body of knowledge. This view of educational outcomes is needed if schools and education systems are to be encouraged to focus on modern challenges.

AN OVERVIEW OF WHAT IS BEING ASSESSED IN EACH DOMAIN

Figure A presents a definition of the four domains assessed in PISA 2003. The definitions all emphasise functional knowledge and skills that allow one to participate actively in society. Such participation requires more than just being able to carry out tasks imposed externally by, for example, an employer. It also means being equipped to take part in decision-making processes. In the more complex tasks in OECD/PISA, students will be asked to reflect on and evaluate material, not just to answer questions that have single "correct" answers.

Figure A ■ **Definitions of the domains**

- Mathematical Literacy

  An individual's capacity to identify and understand the role that mathematics plays in the world, to make well-founded judgements and to use and engage with mathematics in ways that meet the needs of that individual's life as a constructive, concerned and reflective citizen.

- Reading Literacy

  An individual's capacity to understand, use and reflect on written texts, in order to achieve one's goals, to develop one's knowledge and potential and to participate in society.

- Scientific Literacy

  The capacity to use scientific knowledge, to identify questions and to draw evidence-based conclusions in order to understand and help make decisions about the natural world and the changes made to it through human activity.

- Problem Solving Skills

  An individual's capacity to use cognitive processes to confront and resolve real, cross-disciplinary situations where the solution path is not immediately obvious and where the literacy domains or curricular areas that might be applicable are not within a single domain of mathematics, science or reading.

Mathematical literacy (elaborated in Chapter One) is concerned with the ability of students to analyse, reason, and communicate ideas effectively as they pose, formulate, solve, and interpret solutions to mathematical problems in a variety of situations. Mathematical literacy is assessed in relation to:

- The mathematical *content*, as defined mainly in terms of four "overarching ideas" (*quantity*, *space and shape*, *change and relationships*, and *uncertainty*) and only secondarily in relation to "curricular strands" (such as numbers, algebra and geometry).

- The *process* of mathematics as defined by general mathematical competencies. These include the use of mathematical language, modelling and problem-solving skills. Such skills, however, are not separated out in different test items, since it is assumed that a range of competencies will be needed to perform any given mathematical task. Rather, questions are organised in terms of "competency clusters" defining the type of thinking skill needed.

- The *situations* in which mathematics is used, based on their distance to the students. The framework identifies five situations: personal, educational, occupational, public and scientific.

Reading literacy (elaborated in Chapter Two) is defined in terms of students' ability to understand, use and reflect on written text to achieve their purposes. This aspect of literacy has been well established by previous surveys such as the International Adult Literacy Survey (IALS), but is taken further in OECD/PISA by the introduction of an "active" element – the capacity not just to understand a text but to reflect on it, drawing on one's own thoughts and experiences. Reading literacy is assessed in relation to:

- The *text format*. Often students' reading assessments have focused on *continuous texts* or prose organised in sentences and paragraphs. OECD/PISA will in addition introduce *non-continuous texts* that present information in other ways, such as in lists, forms, graphs, or diagrams. It will also distinguish between a range of prose forms, such as narration, exposition and argumentation. These distinctions are based on the principle that individuals will encounter a range of written material in their work related adult life (*e.g.*, applications, forms, advertisements), and that it is not sufficient to be able to read a limited number of types of text typically encountered in school.

- The *reading processes (aspects)*. Students will not be assessed on the most basic reading skills, as it is assumed that most 15-year-olds will have acquired these. Rather, they will be expected to demonstrate their proficiency in retrieving information, forming a broad general understanding of the text, interpreting it, reflecting on its contents and reflecting on its form and features.

- The *situation* defined by the use for which the text was constructed. For example, a novel, personal letter or biography is written for people's personal use; official documents or announcements for public use; a manual or report for occupational use; and a textbook or worksheet for educational use. Since some groups may perform better in one reading situation than in another, it is desirable to include a range of types of reading in the assessment items.

Scientific literacy (elaborated in Chapter Three) is defined as the ability to use scientific knowledge and processes not only to understand the natural world but to participate in decisions that affect it. Scientific literacy is assessed in relation to:

- *Scientific knowledge or concepts*, which constitute the links that aid understanding of related phenomena. In OECD/PISA, while the concepts are the familiar ones relating to physics, chemistry, biological sciences and earth and space sciences, they will need to be applied to the content of the items and not just recalled.

- *Scientific processes*, centred on the ability to acquire, interpret and act upon evidence. Three such processes present in OECD/PISA relate to: *i)* describing, explaining and predicting scientific phenomena, *ii)* understanding scientific investigation, and *iii)* interpreting scientific evidence and conclusions.

- *Scientific situations or context* in which scientific knowledge and the use of scientific processes are applied. The framework identifies three main areas: science in life and health, science in Earth and environment, and science in technology.

Problem solving (elaborated in Chapter Four) is defined as the ability to use cognitive processes to solve real cross-disciplinary problems where neither the solution path nor the applicable literacy domains or curricular areas are immediately obvious. Problem solving is assessed in relation to:

- The *problem type* covering the problem solving processes including decision making, system analysis and design, and trouble shooting applied in specific *problem context*, usually distinct from the classroom setting or school's curricula and involving personal life, work and leisure, and community and society.

- *The problem solving processes*, which involve understanding the nature of the problem, characterising it, representing it, solving it, reflecting on it and communicating its results.

- The *situations* or *problem context* from students' real-life setting in which the problem types will be applied.

HOW THE ASSESSMENT IN 2003 WILL TAKE PLACE AND HOW RESULTS WILL BE REPORTED

Similar to PISA 2000, the PISA 2003 assessment consists of paper-and-pencil instruments for reasons of feasibility. Other forms of assessments are being explored for subsequent cycles. The assessment includes a variety of types of questions. Some require students to select or produce simple responses that can be directly compared with a single correct answer, such as multiple-choice or closed constructed-response items. These questions have either a correct or incorrect answer and often assess lower-order skills. Others are more constructive, requiring students to develop their own responses designed to measure broader constructs than those captured by more traditional surveys, allowing for a wider range of acceptable responses and more complex marking that can include partially correct responses.

Literacy in OECD/PISA is assessed through units consisting of a stimulus (*e.g.*, text, table, chart, figures, etc.) followed by a number of tasks associated with this common stimulus. This is an important feature, allowing questions to go into greater depth than they could if each question introduced a wholly new context. It allows time for the student to digest material that can then be used to assess multiple aspects of performance.

Results from PISA 2000 were reported through scales with an average score of 500 and a standard deviation of 100 for all three domains, which means that two-thirds of students across OECD countries scored between 400 and 600 points. These scores represent degrees of proficiency in a particular aspect of literacy. As reading literacy was the major domain in 2000, the reading scales were divided into five levels of knowledge and skills. The main advantage of this approach is that it describes what students can do by associating the tasks with levels of difficulty. Additionally, results were also presented through three sub-scales of reading: retrieving information, interpreting texts, and reflection and evaluation. A proficiency scale was also available for mathematical and scientific literacy, though without levels thus recognising the limitation of the data from minor domains. PISA 2003 will now build upon this approach by specifying levels for the mathematical literacy scale, following a similar approach to what was done in reading. Additionally, PISA 2003 intends to present trend results for reading, mathematical and scientific literacy as well as a new reporting scale for problem solving as a cross-curricular competency. Similar to the process used in PISA 2000 to report reading outcomes, PISA 2003 is likely to present mathematical literacy results through more than one sub-scale.

THE CONTEXT QUESTIONNAIRES AND THEIR USE

To gather contextual information, OECD/PISA asks students and the principals of their schools to respond to background questionnaires of around 20 to 30 minutes in length. These questionnaires[2] are central to the analysis of results in terms of a range of student and school characteristics.

The questionnaires will seek information about:

- the students and their family backgrounds, including the economic, social and cultural capital of students and their families;

- aspects of students' lives, such as their attitudes to learning, their habits and life inside school and their family environment;

- aspects of schools, such as the quality of the schools' human and material resources, public and private control and funding, decision-making processes and staffing practices;

- the context of instruction, including institutional structures and types, class size and the level of parental involvement;

- strategies of self-regulated learning, motivational preferences and goal orientations, self-related cognition mechanisms, action control strategies, preferences for different types of learning situations, learning styles and social skills required for co-operative learning;

- aspects of learning and instruction in mathematics, including students' motivation, engagement and confidence with mathematics, and the impact of learning strategies on achievement related to the teaching and learning of mathematics.

---

2. The questionnaires from PISA 2000 are available through the Web address *www.pisa.oecd.org.*

Two additional questionnaires are offered as international options:

- A *computer familiarity questionnaire* focusing on: *i)* availability and use of information technology (IT), including the location where IT is mostly used as well as the type of use; *ii)* IT confidence and attitudes, including self-efficacy and attitudes towards computers; and *iii)* learning background of IT, focusing on where students learned to use computers and the Internet.

- An *educational career questionnaire* to collect data on aspects of the students' educational career in three areas: *i)* students' past education including grade repetition, interruptions of schooling, changes of schools and changes of study programme; *ii)* students' current education on aspects involving mathematics, focusing on the type of mathematics classes and the teachers' marks; and *iii)* students' future education and occupation, focusing on expected education level and expected occupation at the age of 30.

The contextual information collected through the student and school questionnaires comprises only a part of the total amount of information available to OECD/PISA. Indicators describing the general structure of the education systems (their demographic and economic contexts – for example, costs, enrolments, school and teacher characteristics, and some classroom processes) and their effect on labour market outcomes are already routinely developed and applied by the OECD.

COLLABORATIVE DEVELOPMENT OF OECD/PISA AND ITS ASSESSMENT FRAMEWORKS

OECD/PISA represents a collaborative effort among the OECD Member governments to provide a new kind of assessment of student achievement on a recurring basis. The assessments are developed co-operatively, agreed by participating countries, and implemented by national organisations. The constructive co-operation of students, teachers and principals in participating schools has been crucial to the success of OECD/PISA during all stages of the development and implementation.

A *Board of Participating Countries*, representing all nations at the senior policy levels, determines the policy priorities for OECD/PISA in the context of OECD objectives and oversees adherence to these priorities during the implementation of the programme. This includes setting priorities for the development of indicators, for the establishment of the assessment instruments and for the reporting of the results. Experts from participating countries also serve on working groups charged with linking the OECD/PISA policy objectives with the best internationally available technical expertise in the different assessment domains. By participating in these expert groups, countries ensure that the instruments are internationally valid and take into account the cultural and educational contexts in OECD Member countries. They also ensure that the assessment materials have strong measurement properties, and that the instruments emphasise authenticity and educational validity.

Participating countries implement OECD/PISA at the national level, through National Project Managers (NPM), subject to the agreed administration procedures. National Project Managers play a vital role in ensuring that implementation is of high quality, and verify and evaluate the survey results, analyses, reports and publications.

The design and implementation of the surveys, within the framework established by the Board of Participating Countries, is the responsibility of an *international consortium* led by the Australian Council for Educational Research (ACER). Other partners in this consortium include the National Institute for Educational Measurement (CITO) in the Netherlands, WESTAT and the Educational Testing Service (ETS) in the United States, and the National Institute for Educational Policy Research (NIER) in Japan.

The OECD Secretariat has overall managerial responsibility for the programme, monitors its implementation on a day-to-day basis, acts as the secretariat for the Board of Participating Countries, builds consensus among countries and serves as the interlocutor between the Board of Participating Countries and the international consortium charged with implementation. The OECD Secretariat is also responsible for the production of the indicators, and the analysis and preparation of the international reports and publications in co-operation with the OECD/PISA consortium, in close consultation with Member countries both at the policy level (Board of Participating Countries) and at the implementation level (National Project Managers).

The development of the OECD/PISA frameworks has been a continuous effort since the programme was created in 1997 and can be described as a sequence of the following steps:

- development of a working definition for the assessment domain and description of the assumptions that underlie that definition;

- evaluation of how to organise the tasks constructed in order to report to policy makers and researchers on student achievement in the domain; identification of key characteristics that should be taken into account when constructing assessment tasks for international use;

- operationalisation of key characteristics that will be used in test construction, with definitions based on existing literature and experience in conducting other large-scale assessments;

- validation of the variables and assessment of the contribution each makes to understanding task difficulty across the various participating countries;

- preparation of an interpretative scheme for the results.

While the main benefit of constructing and validating a framework for each of the domains is improved measurement, there are other potential benefits:

- A framework provides a common language and a vehicle for discussing the purpose of the assessment and what it is trying to measure. Such a discussion encourages the development of a consensus around the framework and the measurement goals.

- An analysis of the kinds of knowledge and skills associated with successful performance provides a basis for establishing standards or levels of proficiency. As the understanding of what is being measured and the ability to interpret scores along a particular scale evolve, an empirical basis for communicating a richer body of information to various constituencies can be developed.

- Identifying and understanding particular variables that underlie successful performance further the ability to evaluate what is being measured and to make changes to the assessment over time.

- The understanding of what is being measured and its connection to what we say about students provides an important link between public policy, assessment and research which, in turn, enhances the usefulness of the data collected. ⌋

Mathematical Literacy

The aim of the OECD/PISA assessment is to develop indicators of the extent to which the educational systems in participating countries have prepared 15-year-olds to play constructive roles as citizens in society. Rather than being limited to the curriculum content students have learned, the assessments focus on determining if students can use what they have learned in the situations they are likely to encounter in their daily lives.

DEFINITION OF THE DOMAIN

The OECD/PISA mathematical literacy domain is concerned with the capacities of students to analyse, reason, and communicate ideas effectively as they pose, formulate, solve, and interpret mathematical problems in a variety of situations. The OECD/PISA assessment focuses on real-world problems, moving beyond the kinds of situations and problems typically encountered in school classrooms. In real-world settings, citizens regularly face situations when shopping, travelling, cooking, dealing with their personal finances, judging political issues, etc. in which the use of quantitative or spatial reasoning or other mathematical competencies would help clarify, formulate or solve a problem. Such uses of mathematics are based on the skills learned and practised through the kinds of problems that typically appear in school textbooks and classrooms. However, they demand the ability to apply those skills in a less structured context, where the directions are not so clear, and where the student must make decisions about what knowledge may be relevant, and how it might usefully be applied.

OECD/PISA mathematical literacy deals with the extent to which 15-year-olds can be regarded as informed, reflective citizens and intelligent consumers. Citizens in every country are increasingly confronted with a myriad of tasks involving quantitative, spatial, probabilistic or other mathematical concepts. For example, media outlets (newspapers, magazines, television, and the Internet) are filled with information in the form of tables, charts and graphs about such subjects as weather, economics, medicine and sports, to name a few. Citizens are bombarded with information on issues such as "global warming and the greenhouse effect", "population growth", "oil slicks and the seas", "the disappearing countryside". Last but not least, citizens are confronted with the need to read forms, to interpret bus and train timetables, to successfully carry out transactions involving money, to determine the best buy at the market, etc. OECD/PISA mathematical literacy focuses on the capacity of 15-year-olds (the age when many students are completing their formal compulsory mathematics learning) to use their mathematical knowledge and understanding to help make sense of these issues and to carry out the resulting tasks.

The mathematical literacy definition for OECD/PISA is:

> *Mathematical literacy is an individual's capacity to identify and understand the role that mathematics plays in the world, to make well-founded judgements and to use and engage with mathematics in ways that meet the needs of that individual's life as a constructive, concerned and reflective citizen.*

Some explanatory remarks may help to further clarify this domain definition.

Mathematical literacy...

The term "mathematical literacy" has been chosen to emphasise mathematical knowledge put to functional use in a multitude of different situations in varied, reflective and insight-based ways. Of course, for such use to be possible and viable, a great deal of fundamental mathematical knowledge and skills are needed, and such skills form part of our definition of literacy. Literacy in the linguistic sense presupposes, but cannot be reduced to, a rich vocabulary and a substantial knowledge of grammatical rules, phonetics, orthography, etc. To communicate, humans combine these elements in creative ways in response to each real-world situation encountered. In the same way, mathematical literacy cannot be reduced to, but certainly presupposes, knowledge of mathematical terminology, facts and procedures, as well as skills in performing certain operations and carrying out certain methods. Mathematical literacy involves the creative combining of these elements in response to the demands imposed by the external situation.

... the world...

The term "the world" means the natural, social and cultural setting in which the individual lives. As Freudenthal (1983) stated: "Our mathematical concepts, structures, ideas have been invented as tools to organise the phenomena of the physical, social and mental world" (p. ix).

... to use and engage with...

The term "to use and engage with" is meant to cover using mathematics and solving mathematical problems, and also implies a broader personal involvement through *communicating, relating to, assessing* and even *appreciating and enjoying* mathematics. Thus the definition of mathematical literacy encompasses the functional use of mathematics in a narrow sense as well as preparedness for further study, and the aesthetic and recreational elements of mathematics.

... that individual's life...

The phrase "that individual's life" includes his or her private life, occupational life, and social life with peers and relatives, as well as life as a citizen of a community.

A crucial capacity implied by this notion of mathematical literacy is the ability to pose, formulate, solve, and interpret problems using mathematics within a variety of situations or contexts. The contexts range from purely mathematical ones to contexts in which no mathematical structure is present or apparent at the outset – the problem poser or solver must successfully introduce the mathematical structure. It is also important to emphasise that the definition is not just concerned with knowing mathematics at some minimal level; it is also about doing and using mathematics in situations that range from the everyday to the unusual, from the simple to the complex.

Mathematics related attitudes and emotions such as self-confidence, curiosity, feelings of interest and relevance, and the desire to do or understand things, are not components of the definition of mathematical literacy but nevertheless are important contributors to it. In principle it is possible to possess mathematical literacy without possessing such attitudes and emotions. In practice, however, it is not likely that such literacy is going to be exerted and put into practice by someone who does not have some degree of self-confidence, curiosity, feelings of interest and relevance, and the desire to do or understand things that contain mathematical components. The importance of these attitudes and emotions as correlates of mathematical literacy is recognised. They are not part of the mathematical literacy assessment, but will be addressed in other components of OECD/PISA.

THEORETICAL BASIS FOR THE OECD/PISA MATHEMATICS FRAMEWORK

The OECD/PISA definition of mathematical literacy is consistent with the broad and integrative theory about the structure and use of language as reflected in recent socio-cultural literacy studies. In James Gee's *Preamble to a Literacy Program* (1998), the term "literacy" refers to the human use of language. The ability to read, write, listen and speak a language is the most important tool through which human social activity is mediated. In fact, each human language and use of language has an intricate design tied in complex ways to a variety of functions. For a person to be literate in a language implies that the person knows many of the design resources of the language and is able to use those resources for several different social *functions*. Analogously, considering mathematics as a language implies that students must learn the design features involved in mathematical discourse (the terms, facts, signs and symbols, procedures and skills in performing certain operations in specific mathematical sub-domains, and the structure of those ideas in each sub-domain), and they also must learn to use such ideas to solve non-routine problems in a variety of situations defined in terms of social functions. Note that the design features for mathematics include knowing the basic terms, procedures and concepts commonly taught in schools, and also involve knowing how these features are structured and used. Unfortunately, one can know a good deal about the design features of mathematics without knowing either their structure or how to use those features to solve problems. These scholarly notions involving the interplay of "design features" and "functions" that support the mathematics framework for OECD/PISA can be illustrated via the following example.

Mathematics Example 1: Streetlight

The Town Council has decided to construct a streetlight in a small triangular park so that it illuminates the whole park. Where should it be placed?

This social problem can be solved by following the general strategy used by mathematicians, which the mathematics framework will refer to as *mathematising*. Mathematising can be characterised as having five aspects:

1. Starting with a problem situated in reality;

   Locating where a street light is to be placed in a park.

2. Organising it according to mathematical concepts;

   The park can be represented as a triangle, and illumination from a light as a circle with the street light at its centre.

3. Gradually trimming away the reality through processes such as making assumptions about which features of the problem are important, generalising and formalising (which promote the mathematical features of the situation and transform the real problem into a mathematical problem that faithfully represents the situation);

   The problem is transformed into locating the centre of a circle that circumscribes the triangle.

4. Solving the mathematical problem; and

   Using the fact that the centre of a circle that circumscribes a triangle lies at the point of intersection of the perpendicular bisectors of the triangle's sides, construct the perpendicular bisectors of two sides of the triangle. The point of intersection of the bisectors is the centre of the circle.

5. Making sense of the mathematical solution in terms of the real situation.

   Relating this finding to the real park. Reflecting on this solution and recognising, for example, that if one of the three corners of the park were an obtuse angle, this solution would not be reasonable since the location of the light would be outside the park. Recognising that the location and size of trees in the park are other factors affecting the usefulness of the mathematical solution.

It is these processes that characterise how, in a broad sense, mathematicians often *do mathematics*, how people use mathematics in a variety of current and potential occupations, and how informed and reflective citizens should use mathematics to fully and competently engage with the real world. In fact, learning to *mathematise* should be a primary educational goal for all students.

Today and in the foreseeable future, every country needs mathematically literate citizens to deal with a very complex and rapidly changing society. Accessible information has been growing exponentially, and citizens need to be able to decide how to deal with this information. Social debates increasingly involve quantitative information to support claims. One example of the need for mathematical literacy is the frequent demand for individuals to make judgements and assess the accuracy of conclusions and claims in surveys and studies. Being able to judge the soundness of the claims from such arguments is, and increasingly will be, a critical aspect of being a responsible citizen. The steps of the mathematisation process discussed in this framework are the fundamental elements of using mathematics in such complex situations. Failure to use mathematical notions can result in confused personal decisions, an increased susceptibility to pseudo-sciences, and poorly informed decision-making in professional and public life.

A mathematically literate citizen realises how quickly change is taking place and the consequent need to be open to lifelong learning. Adapting to these changes in a creative, flexible and practical way is a necessary condition for successful citizenship. The skills learned at school will probably not be sufficient to serve the needs of citizens for the majority of their adult life.

The requirements for competent and reflective citizenship also affect the workforce. Workers are less and less expected to carry out repetitive physical chores for all of their working lives. Instead, they are engaged actively in monitoring output from a variety of high-technology machines, dealing with a flood of information, and engaging in team problem solving. The trend is that more and more occupations will require the ability to understand, communicate, use and explain concepts and procedures based on mathematical thinking. The steps of the mathematisation process are the building blocks of this kind of mathematical thinking.

Finally, mathematically literate citizens also develop an appreciation for mathematics as a dynamic, changing and relevant discipline that may often serve their needs.

The operational problem faced by OECD/PISA is how to assess whether 15-year-old students are mathematically literate in terms of their ability to *mathematise*. Unfortunately, in a timed assessment this is difficult because for most complex real situations the full process of proceeding from reality to mathematics and back often involves collaboration and finding appropriate resources, and takes considerable time.

To illustrate *mathematisation* in an extended problem-solving exercise, consider the "Fairground" Example 2 carried out by an eighth grade class of students (Romberg, 1994):

Mathematics Example 2: FAIRGROUND GAMEBOARD

At a fair, players throw coins onto a board chequered with squares. If a coin touches a boundary, it is lost. If it rolls off the board, it is returned. But if the coin lies wholly within a square, the player wins the coin back plus a prize.

What is the probability of winning at this game?

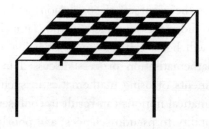

Clearly this exercise is situated in reality. First, the students began by realising that the probability of winning depends on the relative sizes of the squares and the coin (identifying the important variables). Next, to transform the real problem into a mathematical problem, they realised that it might be better to examine the relationship for a single square and a smaller circle (trimming the reality). Then they decided to construct a specific example (using a problem solving heuristic – "if you cannot solve the problem given, solve one you can"). Note that all the following work was done with respect to this specific example, not the board, the prize, etc. In the example, they let the radius of the coin be 3 cm and the side of the squares be 10 cm. They realised that to win, the centre of the coin must be at least 3 cm from each side; otherwise the edge of the coin will fall across the square. The sample space was the square with side 10 cm, and the winning event space was a square with side 4 cm. The relationships are shown in the following diagram (Figure 1.1).

Figure 1.1 ■ **A winning toss and a losing toss (on the left) and the sample and event spaces (on the right)**

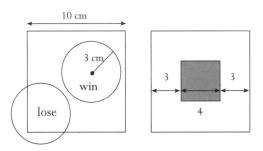

The probability of winning was obtained from the ratio of the area of the sample and event space squares (for the example p = 16/100). Then the students examined coins of other sizes, and generalised the problem by expressing its solution in algebraic terms. Finally the students extended this finding to work out the relative sizes of the coin and squares for a variety of practical situations; they constructed boards and empirically tested results (making sense of the mathematical solution in terms of the real situation).

Note that each of the five aspects of *mathematisation* is apparent in this solution. Although the problem is complex, all 15-year-old students should understand the mathematical features needed to solve the problem. However, note that in this class the students worked together on this exercise for three days.

Ideally, to judge whether 15-year-old students can use their accumulated mathematical knowledge to solve mathematical problems they encounter in their world, one would collect information about their ability to *mathematise* such complex situations. Clearly this is impractical. Instead, OECD/PISA has chosen to prepare items to assess different parts of this process. The following section describes the strategy chosen to create a set of test items in a balanced manner so that a selected sample of these items will cover the five aspects of *mathematising*. The aim is to use the responses to those items to locate students on a scale of proficiency in the OECD/PISA construct of mathematical literacy.

ORGANISATION OF THE DOMAIN

The OECD/PISA mathematics framework provides the rationale for, and the description of, an assessment of the extent to which 15-year-olds can handle mathematics in a well-founded manner when confronted with real-world problems, or, in more general terms, an assessment of how mathematically literate 15-year-olds are. To describe the domain that is assessed more clearly, three components must be distinguished:

- the *situations or contexts* in which the problems are located,
- the *mathematical content* that has to be used to solve the problems, organised by certain overarching *ideas*, and, most importantly,
- the *competencies* that have to be activated in order to connect the real world, in which the problems are generated, with mathematics, and thus to solve the problems.

These components are represented in visual form in Figure 1.2. An explanation of each is provided afterwards.

Figure 1.2 ■ **The components of the mathematics domain**

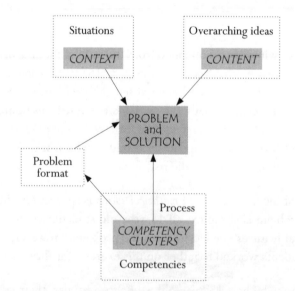

The extent of a person's mathematical literacy is seen in the way he or she uses mathematical knowledge and skills in solving problems. Problems (and their solution) may occur in a variety of "situations or contexts" within the experience of an individual. OECD/PISA problems draw from the real world in two ways. First, problems exist within some broad situations that are relevant to the student's life. The situations form part of the real world and are indicated by a big square in the upper left of the picture. Next, within that situation, problems have a more specific context. This is represented by the small square within the situations square.

In the above examples the situation is the local community, and the contexts are lighting in a park (Example 1), and a fairground checkerboard game (Example 2).

The next component of the real world that has to be considered when thinking about mathematical literacy is the mathematical content that a person might bring to bear in solving a problem. The *mathematical content* can be illustrated by four categories that encompass the kinds of problems that arise through interaction with day-to-day phenomena, and that are based on a conception of the ways in which mathematical content presents itself to people. For PISA assessment purposes, these are called "overarching ideas": *quantity*, *space and shape*, *change and relationships*, and *uncertainty*. This is somewhat different from an approach to content that would be familiar from the perspective of mathematics instruction and the curricular strands typically taught in schools. However, the overarching ideas together broadly encompass the range of mathematical topics that students are expected to have learned. The overarching ideas are represented by the big square in the upper right of the diagram in Figure 1.2. From the overarching ideas the content used in solving a problem is extracted. This is represented by the smaller square within the overarching ideas square.

The arrows going from the "context" and "content" to the problem show how the real world (including mathematics) makes up a problem.

The park problem (Example 1) involves geometrical knowledge related to the ideas of space and shape, and the fairground problem (Example 2) involves (at least in its initial stages) dealing with uncertainty and applying knowledge of probability.

The mathematical processes that students apply as they attempt to solve problems are referred to as *mathematical competencies*. Three *competency clusters* encapsulate the different cognitive processes that are needed to solve various kinds of problems. These clusters reflect the way that mathematical processes are typically employed when solving problems that arise as students interact with their world, and will be described in detail in later sections.

Thus the process component of this framework is represented in first by the large square, representing the general mathematical competencies, and a smaller square that represents the three competency clusters. The particular competencies needed to solve a problem will be related to the nature of the problem, and the competencies used will be reflected in the solution found. This interaction is represented by the arrow from the competency clusters to the problem and its solution.

The remaining arrow goes from the competency clusters to the problem format. The competencies employed in solving a problem are related to the form of the problem and its precise demands.

It should be emphasised that the three components just described are of different natures. While situations or contexts define the real-world problem areas, and overarching ideas reflect the way in which we look at the world with "mathematical glasses", the competencies are the core of mathematical literacy. Only when certain competencies are available to students will they be in a position to successfully solve given problems. Assessing mathematical literacy includes assessing to what extent students possess mathematical competencies they can productively apply in problem situations.

In the following sections, these three components are described in more detail.

Situations or contexts

An important aspect of mathematical literacy is engagement with mathematics: using and doing mathematics in a variety of situations. It has been recognised that in dealing with issues that lend themselves to a mathematical treatment, the choice of mathematical methods and representations is often dependent on the situations in which the problems are presented.

The situation is the part of the student's world in which the tasks are placed. It is located at a certain distance from the students. For OECD/PISA, the closest situation is the student's personal life; next is school life, work life and leisure, followed by the local community and society as encountered in daily life. Furthest away are scientific situations. Four situation-types will be defined and used for problems to be solved: personal, educational/occupational, public, and scientific.

The context of an item is its specific setting within a situation. It includes all the detailed elements used to formulate the problem.

Consider the following example:

Mathematics Example 3: SAVINGS ACCOUNT

1000 zed is put into a savings account at a bank. There are two choices: one can get an annual rate of 4% OR one can get an immediate 10 zed bonus from the bank, and a 3% annual rate. Which option is better after one year? After two years?

The situation of this item is "finance and banking", which is a situation from the local community and society that OECD/PISA would classify as "public". The context of this item concerns money (zeds) and interest rates for a bank account.

Note that this kind of problem is one that could be part of the actual experience or practice of the participant in some real-world setting. It provides an *authentic* context for the use of mathematics, since the application of mathematics in this context would be genuinely directed to solving the problem[1]. This can be contrasted with problems frequently seen in school mathematics texts, where the main purpose is to practise the mathematics involved rather than to use mathematics to solve a real problem. This *authenticity* in the use of mathematics is an important aspect of the design and analysis of items for OECD/PISA, strongly related to the definition of mathematical literacy.

It should also be noted that there are some made-up elements of the problem – the money involved is fictitious. This fictitious element is introduced to ensure that students from certain countries are not given an unfair advantage.

The situation and context of a problem can also be considered in terms of the distance between the problem and the mathematics involved. If a task refers only to mathematical objects, symbols or structures, and makes no reference to matters outside the mathematical world, the context of the task is considered as intra-mathematical, and the task will be classified as belonging to the "scientific" situation-type. A limited range of such tasks will be included in OECD/PISA, where the close link between the problem and the underlying mathematics is made explicit in the problem context. More typically, problems encountered in the day-to-day experience of the student are not stated in explicit mathematical terms. They refer to real-world objects. These task contexts are called "extra-mathematical", and the student must translate these problem contexts into a mathematical form. Generally speaking, OECD/PISA puts an emphasis on tasks that might be encountered in some real-world situation and possess an authentic context for the use of mathematics that influences the solution and its interpretation. Note that this does not preclude the inclusion of tasks in which the context is hypothetical, as long as the context has some real elements, is not too far removed from a real-world situation, and for which the use of mathematics to solve the problem would be authentic. Example 4 shows a problem with a hypothetical context that is "extra-mathematical":

Mathematics Example 4: COINAGE SYSTEM

Would it be possible to establish a coinage system based on only the denominations 3 and 5? More specifically, what amounts could be reached on that basis? Would such a system be desirable?

This problem derives its quality not primarily from its closeness to the real world, but from the fact that it is mathematically interesting and calls on competencies that are related to mathematical literacy. The use of mathematics to explain hypothetical scenarios and explore potential systems or situations, even if these are unlikely to be carried out in reality, is one of its most powerful features. Such a problem would be classified as belonging to the "Scientific" situation-type.

---

1. Note that this use of the term "authentic" is not intended to indicate that mathematics items are in some sense genuine and real. OECD/PISA mathematics uses the terms "authentic" to indicate that the use of mathematics is genuinely directed to solving the problem at hand, rather than the problem being merely a vehicle for the purpose of practising some mathematics.

In summary, OECD/PISA places most value on tasks that could be encountered in a variety of real-world situations, and that have a context in which the use of mathematics to solve the problem would be authentic. Problems with extra-mathematical contexts that influence the solution and its interpretation are preferred as a vehicle for assessing mathematical literacy, since these problems are most like those encountered in day-to-day life.

Mathematical content – The four "overarching ideas"

Mathematical concepts, structures and ideas have been invented as tools to organise the phenomena of the natural, social and mental world. In schools, the mathematics curriculum has been logically organised around content strands (*e.g.*, arithmetic, algebra, geometry) and their detailed topics that reflect historically well-established branches of mathematical thinking, and that facilitate the development of a structured teaching syllabus. However, in the real world the phenomena that lend themselves to mathematical treatment do not come so logically organised. Rarely do problems arise in ways and contexts that allow their understanding and solution to be achieved through an application of knowledge from a single content strand. The "fairground" problem described in Example 2 provides an example of a problem that draws on quite diverse mathematical areas.

Since the goal of OECD/PISA is to assess students' capacity to solve real problems, our strategy has been to define the range of content that will be assessed using a phenomenological approach to describing the mathematical concepts, structures or ideas. This means describing content in relation to the phenomena and the kinds of problems for which it was created. This approach ensures a focus in the assessment that is consistent with the domain definition, yet covers a range of content that includes what is typically found in other mathematics assessments and in national mathematics curricula.

A phenomenological organisation for mathematical content is not new. Two well known publications: *On the shoulders of giants: New approaches to numeracy* (Steen, 1990) and *Mathematics: The science of patterns* (Devlin, 1994) have described mathematics in this manner. However, various ways of labelling the approach and naming the different phenomenological categories have been used. Suggestions for labelling the approach have included "deep ideas", "big ideas", or "fundamental ideas"; "overarching concepts", "overarching ideas", "underlying concepts" or "major domains"; or "problematique". In the mathematics framework for OECD/PISA 2003, the label "overarching ideas" will be used.

There are many possible mathematical overarching ideas. The above mentioned publications alone refer to pattern, dimension, quantity, uncertainty, shape, change, counting, reasoning and communication, motion and change, symmetry and regularity, and position. Which should be used for the OECD/PISA mathematics framework? For the purpose of focusing the mathematical literacy domain, it is important to make a selection of problem areas that grows out of historical developments in mathematics, that encompasses sufficient variety and depth to reveal the essentials of mathematics, and that also represents or includes the conventional mathematical curricular strands in an acceptable way.

For centuries mathematics was predominantly the science of numbers, together with relatively concrete geometry. The period up to 500 BC in Mesopotamia, Egypt and China saw the origin of the concept of number. Operations with numbers and quantities, including quantities resulting from geometrical measurements, were developed. From 500 BC to 300 AD was the era of Greek mathematics, which focused primarily on the study of geometry as an axiomatic theory. The Greeks were responsible for redefining mathematics as a unified science of number and shape. The next major change took place between 500 and 1300 AD in the Islamic world, India and China, which established algebra as a branch of mathematics. This founded the study of relationships. With the independent inventions of calculus (the study of change, growth and limit) by Newton and Leibniz in the 17th century, mathematics became an integrated study of number, shape, change and relationships.

The 19th and 20th centuries saw explosions of mathematical knowledge and of the range of phenomena and problems that could be approached by means of mathematics. These include aspects of randomness and indeterminacy. These developments made it increasingly difficult to give simple answers to the question "what is mathematics?" At the time of the new millennium, many see mathematics as the science of patterns (in a general sense). Thus, a choice of overarching ideas can be made that reflects these developments: patterns in *quantity*, patterns in *space and shape*, patterns in *change and relationships* form central and essential concepts for any description of mathematics, and they form the heart of any curriculum, whether at high school, college or university. But to be literate in mathematics means more. Dealing with uncertainty from a mathematical and scientific perspective is essential. For this reason, elements of probability theory and statistics give rise to the fourth overarching idea: *uncertainty*.

The following list of overarching ideas, therefore, is used in OECD/PISA 2003 to meet the requirements of historical development, coverage of the domain, and reflection of the major threads of school curriculum:

- *quantity;*
- *space and shape;*
- *change and relationships;*
- *uncertainty.*

With these four, mathematical content is organised into a sufficient number of areas to ensure a spread of items across the curriculum, but at the same time a number small enough to avoid a too fine division that would work against a focus on problems based in real situations.

The basic conception of an overarching idea is an encompassing set of phenomena and concepts that make sense and can be encountered within and across a multitude of different situations. By its very nature, each overarching idea can be perceived as a sort of general notion dealing with some generalised content dimension. This implies that the overarching ideas cannot be sharply delineated vis-à-vis one another[2]. Rather, each of them represents a certain perspective, or point of view, which can be thought of as possessing a core, a centre of gravity, and somewhat blurred outskirts that allow for intersection with other overarching ideas. In principle, any overarching idea intersects any other overarching idea. The four overarching ideas are summarised in the following section and discussed more fully afterwards.

Quantity

This overarching idea focuses on the need for quantification in order to organise the world. Important aspects include an understanding of relative size, the recognition of numerical patterns, and the use of numbers to represent quantities and quantifiable attributes of real-world objects (counts and measures). Furthermore, *quantity* deals with the processing and understanding of numbers that are represented to us in various ways.

An important aspect of dealing with *quantity* is quantitative reasoning. Essential components of quantitative reasoning are number sense, representing numbers in various ways, understanding the meaning of operations, having a feel for the magnitude of numbers, mathematically elegant computations, mental arithmetic and estimating.

Space and shape

Patterns are encountered everywhere: in spoken words, music, video, traffic, building constructions and art. Shapes can be regarded as patterns: houses, office buildings, bridges, starfish, snowflakes, town plans, cloverleaves, crystals and shadows. Geometric patterns can serve as relatively simple models of many kinds of phenomena, and their study is possible and desirable at all levels (Grünbaum, 1985).

The study of shape and constructions requires looking for similarities and differences when analysing the components of form and recognising shapes in different representations and different dimensions. The study of shapes is closely connected to the concept of "grasping space". This means learning to know, explore and conquer, in order to live, breathe and move with more understanding in the space in which we live (Freudenthal, 1973).

To achieve this requires understanding the properties of objects and their relative positions. We must be aware of how we see things and why we see them as we do. We must learn to navigate through space and through constructions and shapes. This means understanding the relationship between shapes and images or visual representations, such as that between a real city and photographs and maps of the same city. It includes also understanding how

---

2. And, of course, neither can traditional mathematics content strands.

three-dimensional objects can be represented in two dimensions, how shadows are formed and must be interpreted, what perspective is and how it functions.

Change and relationships

Every natural phenomenon is a manifestation of change, and the world around us displays a multitude of temporary and permanent relationships among phenomena. Examples are organisms changing as they grow, the cycle of seasons, the ebb and flow of tides, cycles of unemployment, weather changes and stock exchange indices. Some of these change processes involve and can be described or modelled by straightforward mathematical functions: linear, exponential, periodic or logistic, either discrete or continuous. But many relationships fall into different categories, and data analysis is often essential to determine the kind of relationship that is present. Mathematical relationships often take the shape of equations or inequalities, but relations of a more general nature (*e.g.*, equivalence, divisibility, inclusion, to mention but a few) may appear as well.

Functional thinking – that is, thinking in terms of and about relationships – is one of the most fundamental disciplinary aims of the teaching of mathematics (MAA, 1923). Relationships may be given a variety of different representations, including symbolic, algebraic, graphical, tabular and geometrical. Different representations may serve different purposes and have different properties. Hence translation between representations often is of key importance in dealing with situations and tasks.

Uncertainty

The present "information society" offers an abundance of information, often presented as accurate, scientific and with a degree of certainty. However, in daily life we are confronted with uncertain election results, collapsing bridges, stock market crashes, unreliable weather forecasts, poor predictions for population growth, economic models that don't align, and many other demonstrations of the uncertainty of our world.

Uncertainty is intended to suggest two related topics: data and chance. These phenomena are respectively the subject of mathematical study in statistics and probability. Relatively recent recommendations concerning school curricula are unanimous in suggesting that statistics and probability should occupy a much more prominent place than has been the case in the past (Committee of Inquiry into the Teaching of Mathematics in Schools, 1982; LOGSE, 1990; MSEB, 1990; NCTM, 1989; NCTM, 2000).

Specific mathematical concepts and activities that are important in this area are collecting data, data analysis and display / visualisation, probability and inference.

We now turn to the most important aspect of the mathematics framework: a discussion of the competencies that students bring to bear when attempting to solve problems. These are discussed under the broad heading of mathematical processes.

Mathematical processes

Introduction - Mathematisation

OECD/PISA examines the capacities of students to analyse, reason, and communicate mathematical ideas effectively as they pose, formulate, solve and interpret mathematical problems in a variety of situations. Such problem solving requires students to use the skills and competencies they have acquired through schooling and life experiences. In OECD/PISA, a fundamental process that students use to solve real-life problems is referred to as "mathematisation".

Newton might have been describing mathematisation in his major work, "Mathematical Principles of Natural Philosophy" when he wrote: "But our purpose is only to trace out the quantity and properties of this force from the phenomena, and to apply what we discover in some simple cases as principles, by which, in a mathematical way, we may estimate the effects thereof in more involved cases" (Newton, 1687).

The earlier discussion of the theoretical basis for the OECD/PISA mathematics framework outlined a five-step description of mathematisation. These steps are shown in Figure 1.3.

Figure 1.3 ■ **The mathematisation cycle**

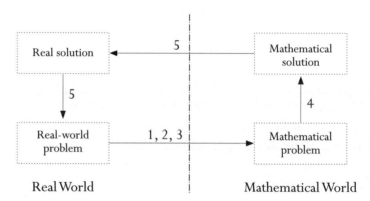

(1) Starting with a problem situated in reality;

(2) Organising it according to mathematical concepts and identifying the relevant mathematics;

(3) Gradually trimming away the reality through processes such as making assumptions, generalising and formalising, which promote the mathematical features of the situation and transform the real-world problem into a mathematical problem that faithfully represents the situation;

(4) Solving the mathematical problem; and

(5) Making sense of the mathematical solution in terms of the real situation, including identifying the limitations of the solution.

As the diagram in Figure 1.3 suggests, the five aspects will be discussed in three stages.

Mathematisation first involves translating the problem from "reality" into mathematics. This process includes activities such as:

- identifying the relevant mathematics with respect to a problem situated in reality;

- representing the problem in a different way; including organising it according to mathematical concepts and making appropriate assumptions;

- understanding the relationships between the language of the problem, and symbolic and formal language needed to understand it mathematically;

- finding regularities, relations, and patterns;

- recognising aspects that are isomorphic with known problems;

- translating the problem into mathematics; *i.e.*, to a mathematical model, (de Lange, 1987, p. 43).

As soon as a student has translated the problem into a mathematical form, the whole process can continue within mathematics. Students will pose questions like: "Is there...?", "If so, how many?", "How do I find...?", using known mathematical skills and concepts. They will attempt to work on their model of the problem situation, to adjust it, to establish regularities, to identify connections and to create a good mathematical argument. This part of the mathematisation process is generally called the deductive part of the modelling cycle (Blum, 1996; Schupp, 1988). However, other than strictly deductive processes may play a part in this stage. This part of the mathematisation process includes:

- using and switching between different representations;

- using symbolic, formal and technical language and operations;

- refining and adjusting mathematical models; combining and integrating models;

- argumentation;

- generalisation.

The last step or steps in solving a problem involve reflecting on the whole mathematisation process and the results. Here students must interpret the results with a critical attitude and validate the whole process. Such reflection takes place at all stages of the process, but it is especially important at the concluding stage. Aspects of this reflecting and validating process are:

- understanding the extent and limits of mathematical concepts;

- reflecting on mathematical arguments, and explaining and justifying results;

- communicating the process and solution;

- critiquing the model and its limits.

This stage is indicated in two places in Figure 1.3 by the label "5", where the mathematisation process passes from the mathematical solution to the real solution, and where this is related back to the original real-world problem.

The competencies

The previous section focused on the major concepts and processes involved in mathematisation. An individual who is to engage successfully in mathematisation within a variety of situations, extra- and intra-mathematical contexts, and overarching ideas, needs to possess a number of mathematical competencies which, taken together, can be seen as constituting comprehensive mathematical competence. Each of these competencies can be possessed at different levels of mastery. Different parts of mathematisation draw differently upon these competencies, both in regard to the particular ones involved and in regard to the required level of mastery. To identify and examine these competencies, OECD/PISA has decided to make use of eight characteristic mathematical competencies that rely, in their present form, on the work of Niss (1999) and his Danish colleagues. Similar formulations may be found in the work of many others (as indicated in Neubrand *et al.*, 2001). Some of the terms used, however, have different usage among different authors.

1. *Thinking and reasoning.* This involves posing questions characteristic of mathematics ("Is there…?", "If so, how many?", "How do we find…?"); knowing the kinds of answers that mathematics offers to such questions; distinguishing between different kinds of statements (definitions, theorems, conjectures, hypotheses, examples, conditioned assertions); and understanding and handling the extent and limits of given mathematical concepts.

2. *Argumentation.* This involves knowing what mathematical proofs are and how they differ from other kinds of mathematical reasoning; following and assessing chains of mathematical arguments of different types; possessing a feel for heuristics ("What can(not) happen, and why?"); and creating and expressing mathematical arguments.

3. *Communication.* This involves expressing oneself, in a variety of ways, on matters with a mathematical content, in oral as well as in written form, and understanding others' written or oral statements about such matters.

4. *Modelling.* This involves structuring the field or situation to be modelled; translating "reality" into mathematical structures; interpreting mathematical models in terms of "reality"; working with a mathematical model; validating the model; reflecting, analysing and offering a critique of a model and its results; communicating about the model and its results (including the limitations of such results); and monitoring and controlling the modelling process.

5. *Problem posing and solving.* This involves posing, formulating, and defining different kinds of mathematical problems (for example "pure", "applied", "open-ended" and "closed"); and solving different kinds of mathematical problems in a variety of ways.

6. *Representation.* This involves decoding and encoding, translating, interpreting and distinguishing between different forms of representation of mathematical objects and situations, and the interrelationships between the various representations; choosing and switching between different forms of representation, according to situation and purpose.

7. *Using symbolic, formal and technical language and operations.* This involves decoding and interpreting symbolic and formal language, and understanding its relationship to natural language; translating from natural language to symbolic/formal language; handling statements and expressions containing symbols and formulae; using variables, solving equations and undertaking calculations.

8. *Use of aids and tools.* This involves knowing about, and being able to make use of, various aids and tools (including information technology tools) that may assist mathematical activity, and knowing about the limitations of such aids and tools.

OECD/PISA does not intend to develop test items that assess the above competencies individually. There is considerable overlap among them, and when using mathematics, it is usually necessary to draw simultaneously on many of the competencies, so that any effort to assess individual ones is likely to result in artificial tasks and unnecessary compartmentalisation of the mathematical literacy domain. The particular competencies students will be able to display will vary considerably among individuals. This is partially because all learning occurs through experiences, "with individual knowledge construction occurring through the processes of interaction, negotiation, and collaboration" (de Corte, Greer, & Verschaffel, 1996, p. 510). OECD/PISA assumes that much of students' mathematics is learned in schools. Understanding of a domain is acquired gradually. More formal and abstract ways of representing and reasoning emerge over time as a consequence of engagement in activities designed to help informal ideas evolve. Mathematical literacy is also acquired through experience involving interactions in a variety of social situations or contexts.

In order to productively describe and report students' capabilities, as well as their strengths and weaknesses from an international perspective, some structure is needed. One way of providing this in a comprehensible and manageable way is to describe clusters of competencies, based on the kinds of cognitive demands needed to solve different mathematical problems.

Competency clusters

OECD/PISA has chosen to describe the cognitive activities that these competencies encompass according to three *competency clusters*: the *reproduction* cluster, the *connections* cluster, and the *reflection* cluster. In the following sections the three clusters are described, and the ways in which the individual competencies are played out in each cluster are discussed.

The reproduction cluster

The competencies in this cluster essentially involve reproduction of practised knowledge. They include those most commonly used on standardised assessments and classroom tests. These competencies are knowledge of facts and of common problem representations, recognition of equivalents, recollection of familiar mathematical objects and properties, performance of routine procedures, application of standard algorithms and technical skills, manipulation of expressions containing symbols and formulae in standard form, and carrying out computations.

1. *Thinking and reasoning.* This involves posing the most basic forms of questions ("how many…?", "how much is…?") and understanding the corresponding kinds of answers ("so many…", "this much…"); distinguishing between definitions and assertions; understanding and handling mathematical concepts in the sorts of contexts in which they were first introduced or have subsequently been practised.

2. *Argumentation.* This involves following and justifying standard quantitative processes, including computational processes, statements and results.

3. *Communication.* This involves understanding and expressing oneself orally and in writing about simple mathematical matters, such as reproducing the names and the basic properties of familiar objects, citing computations and their results, usually not in more than one way.

4. *Modelling.* This involves recognising, recollecting, activating, and exploiting well structured familiar models; interpreting back and forth between such models (and their results) and "reality"; and elementary communication about model results.

5. *Problem posing and solving.* This involves posing and formulating problems by recognising and reproducing practised standard pure and applied problems in closed form; and solving such problems by invoking and using standard approaches and procedures, typically in one way only.

6. *Representation.* This involves decoding, encoding and interpreting familiar, practised standard representations of well known mathematical objects. Switching between representations is involved only when the switching itself is an established part of the representations implied.

7. *Using symbolic, formal and technical language and operations.* This involves decoding and interpreting routine basic symbolic and formal language practised in well known contexts and situations; handling simple statements and expressions containing symbols and formulae, including using variables, solving equations and undertaking calculations by routine procedures.

8. *Use of aids and tools.* This involves knowing about and being able to use familiar aids and tools in contexts, situations and ways close to those in which their use was introduced and practised.

Assessment items measuring the *reproduction* cluster competencies might be described with the following key descriptors: reproducing practised material and performing routine operations.

Examples of reproduction cluster items

Mathematics Example 5
Solve the equation 7x–3 = 13x + 15

Mathematics Example 6
What is the average of 7, 12, 8, 14, 15, 9?

Mathematics Example 7
Write 69% as a fraction.

Mathematics Example 8
Line m is called the circle"s: _____

Mathematics Example 9
1 000 zed is put in a savings account at a bank, with an interest rate of 4%.
How many zed will there be in the account after one year?

In order to clarify the boundary for items from the *reproduction* cluster, the savings account problem described in Example 3 provided an example that does NOT belong to the *reproduction* cluster. This problem will take most students beyond the simple application of a routine procedure, and requires the application of a chain of reasoning and a sequence of computational steps that are not characteristic of the *reproduction* cluster competencies.

The connections cluster

The *connections* cluster competencies build on the *reproduction* cluster competencies in taking problem solving to situations that are not simply routine, but still involve familiar, or quasi-familiar, settings.

In addition to the competencies described for the *reproduction* cluster, for the *connections* cluster the competencies include the following:

1. *Thinking and reasoning.* This involves posing questions ("how do we find…?", "which mathematics is involved…?") and understanding the corresponding kinds of answers (provided by means of tables, graphs, algebra, figures, etc.); distinguishing between definitions and assertions, and between different kinds of assertions; and understanding and handling mathematical concepts in contexts that are slightly different from those in which they were first introduced or have subsequently been practised.

2. *Argumentation.* This involves simple mathematical reasoning without distinguishing between proofs and broader forms of argument and reasoning;

following and assessing chains of mathematical arguments of different types, and possessing a feel for heuristics (*e.g.* "what can or cannot happen, or be the case, and why?", "what do we know, and what do we want to obtain?").

3. *Communication.* This involves understanding and expressing oneself orally and in writing about mathematical matters ranging from reproducing the names and basic properties of familiar objects and explaining computations and their results (usually in more than one way), to explaining matters that include relationships. It also involves understanding others' written or oral statements about such matters.

4. *Modelling.* This involves structuring the field or situation to be modelled; translating "reality" into mathematical structures in contexts that are not too complex but nevertheless different from what students are usually familiar with. It involves also interpreting back and forth between models (and their results) and "reality", including aspects of communication about model results.

5. *Problem posing and solving.* This involves posing and formulating problems beyond the reproduction of practised standard pure and applied problems in closed form; solving such problems by invoking and using standard approaches and procedures, but also more independent problem solving processes in which connections are made between different mathematical areas and modes of representation and communication (schemata, tables, graphs, words, pictures).

6. *Representation.* This involves decoding, encoding and interpreting familiar and less familiar representations of mathematical objects; choosing and switching between different forms of representation of mathematical objects and situations, and translating and distinguishing between different forms of representation.

7. *Using symbolic, formal and technical language and operations.* This involves decoding and interpreting basic symbolic and formal language in less well known contexts and situations, and handling statements and expressions containing symbols and formulae, including using variables, solving equations and undertaking calculations by familiar procedures.

8. *Use of aids and tools.* This involves knowing about and using familiar aids and tools in contexts, situations and ways that are different from those in which their use was introduced and practised.

Items associated with this cluster usually require some evidence of the integration and connection of material from the various overarching ideas, or from different mathematical curriculum strands, or the linking of different representations of a problem.

Assessment items measuring the *connections* cluster of competencies might be described with the following key descriptors: integrating, connecting, and modest extension of practised material.

Examples of connections cluster items

A first example of a *connections* cluster item was given in the "savings account" problem described in Example 3. Other examples of *connections* cluster items follow.

Mathematics Example 10: DISTANCE

Mary lives two kilometres from school, Martin five.

How far do Mary and Martin live from each other?

When this problem was originally presented to teachers, many of them rejected it on the ground that it was too easy – one could easily see that the answer is 3. Another group of teachers argued that this was not a good item because there was no answer – meaning there is not one single numerical answer. A third reaction was that it was not a good item because there were many possible answers, since without further information the most that can be concluded is that they live somewhere between 3 and 7 kilometres apart, and that is not desirable for an item. A small group thought it was an excellent item, because you have to understand the question, it is real problem solving because there is no strategy known to the student, and it is beautiful mathematics, although you have no clue how students will solve the problem. It is this last interpretation that associates the problem with the *connections* cluster of competencies.

Mathematics Example 11: THE OFFICE RENTING

The following two advertisements appeared in a daily newspaper in a country where the units of currency are zeds.

BUILDING A	BUILDING B
Office space available	Office space available
58–95 square metres 475 zeds per month	35–260 square metres 90 zeds per square metre per year
100–120 square metres 800 zeds per month	

If a company is interested in renting an office of 110 square metres in that country for a year, at which office building, A or B, should the company rent the office in order to get the lower price? Show your work. [© IEA/TIMSS]

Mathematics Example 12: THE PIZZA

A pizzeria serves two round pizzas of the same thickness in different sizes. The smaller one has a diameter of 30 cm and costs 30 zeds. The larger one has a diameter of 40 cm and costs 40 zeds. [© PRIM, Stockholm Institute of Education]

Which pizza is better value for money? Show your reasoning.

In both of these problems, students are required to translate a real-world situation into mathematical language, to develop a mathematical model that enables them to make a suitable comparison, to check that the solution fits in with the initial question context and to communicate the result. These are all activities associated with the *connections* cluster.

The reflection cluster

The competencies in this cluster include an element of reflectiveness on the part of the student about the processes needed or used to solve a problem. They relate to students' abilities to plan solution strategies and implement them in problem settings that contain more elements and may be more "original" (or unfamiliar) than those in the *connections* cluster. In addition to the competencies described for the *connections* cluster, for the *reflection* cluster the competencies include the following:

1. *Thinking and reasoning:* This involves posing questions ("how do we find...?", "which mathematics is involved...?", "what are the essential aspects of the problem or situation...?") and understanding the corresponding kinds of answers (provided by tables, graphs, algebra, figures, specification of key points etc.); distinguishing between definitions, theorems, conjectures, hypotheses and assertions about special cases, and reflecting upon or actively articulating these distinctions; understanding and handling mathematical concepts in contexts that are new or complex; and understanding and handling the extent and limits of given mathematical concepts, and generalising results.

2. *Argumentation.* This involves simple mathematical reasoning, including distinguishing between proving and proofs and broader forms of argument and reasoning; following, assessing and constructing chains of mathematical arguments of different types; and using heuristics (*e.g.* "what can or cannot happen, or be the case, and why?", "what do we know, and what do we want to obtain?", "which properties are essential?", "how are the objects related?").

3. *Communication.* This involves understanding and expressing oneself orally and in writing about mathematical matters ranging from reproducing the names and basic properties of familiar objects, and explaining computations and their results (usually in more than one way), to explaining matters that include complex relationships, including logical relationships. It also involves understanding others' written or oral statements about such matters.

4. *Modelling.* This involves structuring the field or situation to be modelled; translating "reality" into mathematical structures in contexts that may be complex or largely different from what students are usually familiar with; interpreting back and forth between models (and their results) and "reality", including aspects of communication about model results: gathering information and data, monitoring the modelling process and validating the resulting model. It also includes reflecting through analysing, offering a critique, and engaging in more complex communication about models and modelling.

5. *Problem posing and solving.* This involves posing and formulating problems well beyond the reproduction of practised standard pure and applied problems in closed form; solving such problems by invoking and using standard approaches and procedures, but also more original problem solving processes in which connections are being made between different mathematical areas and modes of representation and communication (schemata, tables, graphs, words, pictures). It also involves reflecting on strategies and solutions.

6. *Representation.* This involves decoding, encoding and interpreting familiar and less familiar representations of mathematical objects; choosing and switching between different forms of representation of mathematical objects and situations, and translating and distinguishing between different forms of representation. It further involves the creative combination of representations and the invention of non-standard ones.

7. *Using symbolic, formal and technical language and operations.* This involves decoding and interpreting symbolic and formal language practised in unknown contexts and situations, and handling statements and expressions containing symbols and formulae, including using variables, solving equations and undertaking calculations. It also involves the ability to deal with complex statements and expressions and with unfamiliar symbolic or formal language, and to understand and to translate between such language and natural language.

8. *Use of aids and tools.* This involves knowing about and using familiar or unfamiliar aids and tools in contexts, situations and ways that are quite different from those in which their use was introduced and practised. It also involves knowing about limitations of aids and tools.

Assessment items measuring the *reflection* cluster of competencies might be described with the following key descriptors: advanced reasoning, argumentation, abstraction, generalisation, and modelling applied to new contexts.

Examples of reflection cluster items

Mathematics Example 13: FISH GROWTH

Some fish were introduced to a waterway. The graph shows a model of the growth in the combined weight of fish in the waterway.

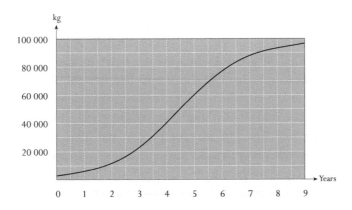

Suppose a fisherman plans to wait a number of years and then start catching fish from the waterway. How many years should the fisherman wait if he or she wishes to maximise the number of fish he or she can catch annually from that year on? Provide an argument to support your answer.

Mathematics Example 14: BUDGET

In a certain country, the national defence budget is $30 million for 1980. The total budget for that year is $500 million. The following year the defence budget is $35 million, while the total budget is $605 million. Inflation during the period covered by the two budgets amounted to 10 per cent.

A. You are invited to give a lecture for a pacifist society. You intend to explain that the defence budget decreased over this period. Explain how you would do this.

B. You are invited to lecture to a military academy. You intend to explain that the defence budget increased over this period. Explain how you would do this.

Source: de Lange and Verhage (1992). Used with permission.

It is clear that Example 13 fits the definition of mathematical problem solving in an authentic context. Students will have to come up with their own strategies and argumentation in a somewhat complex and unfamiliar problem. The complexity lies partly in the need to thoughtfully combine information presented both graphically and in text. Moreover, there is no answer that students can see immediately. They need to interpret the graph, and realise, for instance, that the growth rate reaches its maximum after five years or so. To be successful, students need to reflect on their solution as it emerges and think about the success of their strategy. Furthermore, the problem asks for an argument and an indication of "proof". One possibility is to use the trial and error method: see what happens if you wait only 3 years, for instance, and go on from there. If you wait until the end of the fifth year, you can have a big harvest every year – 20 000 kg of fish. If you can't wait that long, and start to harvest one year earlier, you can catch only 17 000 kg, and if you wait too long (six years), you can only catch 18 000 kg per year. The optimal result is therefore obtained when harvesting commences after five years.

Example 14 has been thoroughly researched with 16-year-old students (de Lange, 1987, pp. 87-90). It illustrates *reflection* cluster problems very well: the students recognised the literacy aspect immediately and quite often were able to do some kind of generalisation, as the heart of the solution lies in recognising that the key mathematical concepts here are absolute and relative growth. Inflation can of course be left out to make the problem more accessible to somewhat younger students without losing the key conceptual ideas behind the problem, but one loses in the complexity and thus in the required mathematisation. Another way to make the item "easier" is to present the data in a table or schema. These mathematisation aspects are then no longer necessary – students can start right away at the heart of the matter.

Figure 1.4 ■ Diagrammatic representation of the competency clusters

Mathematical literacy

The Reproduction Cluster

• Standard representations and definitions

• Routine computations

• Routine procedures

• Routine problem solving

The Connection Cluster

• Modeling

• Standard problem solving translation and interpretation

• Multiple well-defined methods

The Reflection Cluster

• Complex problem-solving and posing

• Reflection and insight

• Original mathematical approach

• Multiple complex methods

• Generalisation

Summary of mathematical processes in OECD/PISA mathematics

Figure 1.4 provides a diagrammatic representation of the competency clusters and summarises the distinctions between them.

It would be possible to use the competency descriptions in the preceding pages to classify mathematics items and thereby to assign them to one of the competency clusters. One way to do this would be to analyse the demands of the item, then to rate each of the eight competencies for that item, according to which of the three clusters provided the most fitting description of item demands in relation to that competency. If any of the competencies were rated as fitting the description for the *reflection* cluster, then the item would be assigned to the *reflection* competency cluster. If not, but one or more of the competencies were rated as fitting the description for the *connections* cluster, then the item would be assigned to that cluster. Otherwise, the item would be assigned to the *reproduction* cluster, since all competencies would have been rated as fitting the competency descriptions for that cluster.

ASSESSING MATHEMATICAL LITERACY

Task characteristics

In the previous sections, the OECD/PISA mathematical literacy domain has been defined and the structure of the assessment framework has been described. This section considers in more detail features of the assessment tasks that will be used to assess students. The nature of the tasks and the item format types are described.

The nature of tasks for OECD/PISA mathematics

OECD/PISA is an international test of the literacy skills of 15-year-olds. All test items used should be suitable for the population of 15-year-old students in OECD countries.

In general, items include of some stimulus material or information, an introduction, the actual question and the required solution. In addition, for items with responses that cannot be automatically coded, a detailed coding scheme will is developed to enable trained markers across the range of participating countries to code the student responses in a consistent and reliable way.

In an earlier section of this framework, the situations to be used for OECD/PISA mathematics items were discussed in some detail. For OECD/PISA 2003, each item is set in one of four situation types: personal, educational/occupational, public and scientific. The items selected for the OECD/PISA 2003 mathematics instruments represent a spread across these situation types.

In addition, item contexts that can be regarded as *authentic* are preferred. That is, OECD/PISA values most highly tasks that could be encountered in real-world situations, and that have a context for which the use of mathematics to solve the problem would be authentic. Problems with extra-mathematical contexts that influence the solution and its interpretation are preferred as vehicles for assessing mathematical literacy.

Items should relate predominantly to the overarching ideas (the phenomenological problem categories) described in the framework. The selection of mathematics test items for OECD/PISA 2003 ensures that the four overarching ideas are well represented.

Items should embody one or more of the mathematical processes that are described in the framework, and should be identified predominantly with one of the competency clusters.

The level of reading required to successfully engage with an item is considered very carefully in the development and selection of items for inclusion in the OECD/PISA 2003 test instrument. The wording of items is as simple and direct as possible. Care is also taken to avoid question contexts that would create a cultural bias.

Items selected for inclusion in the OECD/PISA test instruments represent a broad range of difficulties, to match the expected wide ability range of students participating in the OECD/PISA assessment. In addition, the major classifications of the framework (particularly competency clusters and overarching ideas) should as far as possible be represented with items of a wide range of difficulties. Item difficulties are established in an extensive Field Trial of test items prior to item selection for the main OECD/PISA survey.

Item types

When assessment instruments are devised, the impact of the item type on student performance, and hence on the definition of the construct that is being assessed, must be carefully considered. This issue is particularly pertinent in a project such as OECD/PISA, in which the large-scale cross-national context for testing places serious constraints on the range of feasible item format types.

OECD/PISA will assess mathematical literacy through a combination of items with open constructed-response types, closed constructed-response types and multiple-choice types. About equal numbers of each of these item format types will be used in constructing the test instruments for OECD/PISA 2003.

Based on experience in developing and using test items for OECD/PISA 2000, the multiple-choice type is generally regarded as most suitable for assessing items that would be associated with the *reproduction* and *connections* competency cluster. For an example of this item type, see Example 15, which shows an item that would be associated with the *connections* competency cluster and with a limited number of defined response-options. To solve this problem, students must translate the problem into mathematical terms, devise a model to represent the periodic nature of the context described, and extend the pattern to match the result with one of the given options.

Mathematics Example 15: SEAL

A seal has to breathe even if it is asleep. Martin observed a seal for one hour. At the start of his observation the seal dived to the bottom of the sea and started to sleep. In 8 minutes it slowly floated to the surface and took a breath.

In 3 minutes it was back at the bottom of the sea again and the whole process started over in a very regular way.

After one hour the seal was:

A. at the bottom

B. on its way up

C. breathing

D. on its way down

For some of the higher-order goals and more complex processes, other item types will often be preferred. Closed constructed-response items pose questions similar to multiple-choice items, but students are asked to produce a response that can be easily judged to be either correct or incorrect. For items in this type, guessing is not likely to be a concern, and the provision of distractors (which influence the construct that is being assessed) is not necessary. For example, for the problem in Example 16 there is one correct answer and many possible incorrect answers.

Mathematics Example 16: Rotterdam Marathon

Tegla Loroupe won the 1998 marathon of Rotterdam. "It is easy", she said, "the course was quite flat". Here you see a graph of the differences in elevation of the Rotterdam marathon course:

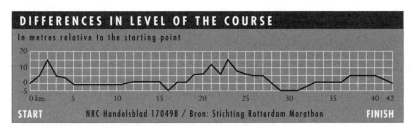

What was the difference between the highest and the lowest points of the course?
_____m

Open constructed-response items require a more extended response from the student, and the process of producing a response frequently involves higher-order cognitive activities. Often such items not only ask the student to produce a response, but also require the student to show the steps taken or to explain how the answer was reached. The key feature of open constructed-response items is that they allow students to demonstrate their abilities by providing solutions at a range of levels of mathematical complexity, exemplified in Example 17.

Mathematics Example 17: INDONESIA

Indonesia lies between Malaysia and Australia. Some data of the population of Indonesia and its distribution over the islands is shown in the following table:

Region	Surface area (Km²)	Percentage of total area	Population in 1980 (millions)	Percentage of total population
Java/Madura	132 187	6.95	91 281	61.87
Sumatra	473 606	24.86	27 981	18.99
Kalimantan (Borneo)	539 460	28.32	6 721	4.56
Sulawesi (Celebes)	189 216	9.93	10 377	7.04
Bali	5 561	0.30	2 470	1.68
Irian Jaya	421 981	22.16	1 145	5.02
TOTAL	1 905 569	100.00	147 384	100.00

One of the main challenges for Indonesia is the uneven distribution of the population over the islands. From the table we can see that Java, which has less than 7% of the total area, has almost 62% of the population.

Design a graph (or graphs) that shows the uneven distribution of the Indonesian population.

Source: de Lange and Verhage (1992). Used with permission.

For OECD/PISA, about one third of the mathematics items will be open constructed-response items. The responses to these items require coding by trained people who implement a coding rubric that may require an element of professional judgement. Because of the potential for disagreement between markers of these items, OECD/PISA will implement marker reliability studies to monitor the extent of disagreement. Experience in these types of studies shows that clear coding rubrics can be developed and reliable scores can be obtained.

OECD/PISA will make some use of a unit format in which several items are linked to common stimulus material. Tasks of this format give students the opportunity to become involved with a context or problem by asking a series of questions of increasing complexity. The first few questions are typically

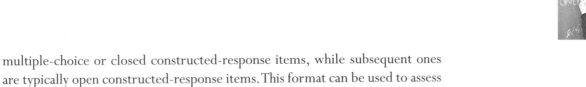

multiple-choice or closed constructed-response items, while subsequent ones are typically open constructed-response items. This format can be used to assess each of the competency clusters.

One reason for the use of common stimulus task formats is that it allows realistic tasks to be devised and the complexity of real-life situations to be reflected in them. Another reason relates to the efficient use of testing time, cutting down on the time required for a student to "get into" the subject matter of the situation. The need to make each scored point independent of others within the task is recognised and taken into account in the design of the OECD/PISA tasks and of the response coding and scoring rubrics. The importance of minimising bias that may result from the use of fewer situations is also recognised.

Assessment structure

The OECD/PISA 2003 test instruments contain a total of 210 minutes of testing time. The selected test items are arranged in seven clusters of items, with each item-cluster representing 30 minutes of testing time. The item-clusters are placed in test booklets according to a rotated test design.

The total testing time for mathematics is distributed as evenly as possible across the four overarching ideas (*quantity*, *space and shape*, *change and relationships*, and *uncertainty*), and the four situations described in the framework (*personal*, *educational / occupational*, *public*, and *scientific*). The proportion of items reflecting the three competency clusters (*reproduction*, *connections* and *reflection*) is about 1:2:1. About one-third of the items is in multiple-choice format type, about one-third in closed constructed-response type, and about one-third in open constructed-response type.

Reporting mathematical proficiency

To summarise data from responses to the OECD/PISA test instruments, a five-level described performance scale will be created (Masters & Forster, 1996; Masters, Adams, & Wilson, 1999). The scale will be created statistically, using an item response modelling approach to scaling ordered outcome data. The overall scale will be used to describe the nature of performance by classifying the student performances of different countries in terms of the five described performance levels, and thus provide a frame of reference for international comparisons.

Consideration will be given to developing a number of separate reporting scales. Such sub-scales could most obviously be based on the three competency clusters, or on the four overarching ideas. Decisions about the development of separate reporting scales will be made on a variety of grounds, including psychometric considerations, following analysis of the data generated by the OECD/PISA assessments. To facilitate these possibilities, it will be necessary to ensure that sufficient items are selected for inclusion in the OECD/PISA test instrument from each potential reporting category. Moreover, items within each such category will need to have a suitably wide range of difficulties.

Mathematical Literacy

The competency clusters described earlier in this framework reflect conceptual categories of broadly increasing cognitive demand and complexity, but do not strictly reflect a hierarchy of student performances based on item difficulty. Conceptual complexity is only one component of item difficulty that influences levels of performance. Others include familiarity, recent opportunity to learn and practice, etc. Thus, a multiple-choice item involving competencies from the *reproduction* cluster (for example, "which of the following is a rectangular parallelepiped?" followed by pictures of a ball, a can, a box, and a square) may be very easy for students who have been taught the meaning of these terms, but very difficult for others because of lack of familiarity with the terminology used. While it is possible to imagine relatively difficult *reproduction* cluster items and relatively easy *reflection* cluster items, and as far as possible items with a range of difficulties within each cluster type should be included, one would expect a broadly positive relationship between competency clusters and item difficulty.

Factors that will underpin increasing levels of item difficulty and mathematical proficiency include the following:

- The kind and degree of interpretation and reflection needed. This includes the nature of demands arising from the problem context; the extent to which the mathematical demands of the problem are apparent or to which students must impose their own mathematical construction on the problem; and the extent to which insight, complex reasoning and generalisation are required.

- The kind of representation skills that are necessary, ranging from problems where only one mode of representation is used, to problems where students have to switch between different modes of representation or to find appropriate modes of representation themselves.

- The kind and level of mathematical skill required, ranging from single-step problems requiring students to reproduce basic mathematical facts and perform simple computation processes through to multi-step problems involving more advanced mathematical knowledge, complex decision-making, information processing, and problem solving and modelling skills.

- The kind and degree of mathematical argumentation that is required, ranging from problems where no arguing is necessary at all, through problems where students may apply well-known arguments, to problems where students have to create mathematical arguments or to understand other people's argumentation or judge the correctness of given arguments or proofs.

At the lowest described proficiency level, students typically carry out single-step processes that involve recognition of familiar contexts and mathematically well-formulated problems, reproducing well-known mathematical facts or processes, and applying simple computational skills.

At higher proficiency levels, students typically carry out more complex tasks involving more than a single processing step. They also combine different pieces of information or interpret different representations of mathematical concepts or information, recognising which elements are relevant and important and how they relate to one another. They typically work with given mathematical models or formulations, which are frequently in algebraic form, to identify solutions, or they carry out a small sequence of processing or calculation steps to produce a solution.

At the highest proficiency level, students take a more creative and active role in their approach to mathematical problems. They typically interpret more complex information and negotiate a number of processing steps. They produce a formulation of a problem and often develop a suitable model that facilitates its solution. Students at this level typically identify and apply relevant tools and knowledge in an unfamiliar problem context. They likewise demonstrate insight in identifying a suitable solution strategy, and display other higher-order cognitive processes such as generalisation, reasoning and argumentation to explain or communicate results.

Aids and tools

The OECD/PISA policy with regard to the use of calculators and other tools is that students should be free to use them as they are normally used in school.

This represents the most authentic assessment of what students can achieve, and will provide the most informative comparison of the performance of education systems. A system's choice to allow students to access and use calculators is no different, in principle, from other instructional policy decisions that are made by systems and are not controlled by OECD/PISA.

Students who are used to having a calculator available to assist them in answering questions will be disadvantaged if this resource is taken away.

SUMMARY

The aim of the OECD/PISA study is to develop indicators that show how effectively countries have prepared their 15-year-olds to become active, reflective and intelligent citizens from the perspective of their uses of mathematics. To achieve this, OECD/PISA has developed assessments that focus on determining the extent to which students can use what they have learned.

This framework provides a definition of mathematical literacy, and sets the context for the assessment of mathematical literacy in 2003 that will permit OECD countries to monitor some important outcomes of their education systems. The definition of mathematical literacy chosen for this framework is consistent with those definitions for literacy in reading and scientific literacy, and with the OECD/PISA orientation of assessing students' capacities to become active and contributing members of society.

The major components of the mathematics framework, consistent with the other OECD/PISA frameworks, include contexts for the use of mathematics, mathematical content and mathematical processes, each of which flows directly out of the literacy definition. The discussions of context and content emphasise features of the problems that confront students as citizens, while the discussions of processes emphasise the competencies that students bring to bear to solve those problems. These competencies have been grouped into three so-called "competency clusters" to facilitate a rational treatment of the way complex cognitive processes are adressed within a structured assessment program.

The emphasis of the OECD/PISA mathematics assessments on using mathematical knowledge and understanding to solve problems that arise out of day-to-day experience embodies an ideal that is achieved to varying degrees in different education systems around the world. The OECD/PISA assessments attempt to provide a variety of mathematical problems with varying degrees of built-in guidance and structure, but pushing towards authentic problems where students must do the thinking themselves.

ADDITIONAL EXAMPLES

In this section, a number of mathematics items are presented in order to illustrate aspects of the OECD/PISA mathematics framework. The items are accompanied by commentary that is intended to describe elements of the items in relation to the framework.

This is the third set of sample mathematics items provided by the OECD. Seven units (comprising a total of 14 items) were published in *Measuring Student Knowledge and Skills* (OECD, 2000). A further five units (comprising a total of 11 items) were published in *Sample Tasks from the PISA 2000 Assessment* (OECD, 2002a).

Thirteen complete units are included here, comprising a total of 27 items. Each of these items was used in the field trial in 2002, as part of the item development process for the 2003 PISA main study. For a variety of reasons, largely related to the need for a complex balance of features in constructing the final test instruments, these items could not be included in the main study item selection. Some of them have measurement properties that make them less than ideal for use in an international test, but they are nevertheless useful for illustrative purposes and possibly for classroom use.

Mathematics Unit 1
LIGHTHOUSE

Lighthouses are towers with a light beacon on top. Lighthouses assist sea ships in finding their way at night when they are sailing close to the shore.

A lighthouse beacon sends out light flashes with a regular fixed pattern. Every lighthouse has its own pattern.

In the diagram below you see the pattern of a certain lighthouse. The light flashes alternate with dark periods.

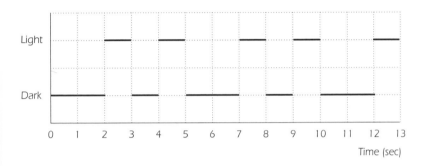

It is a regular pattern. After some time the pattern repeats itself. The time taken by one complete cycle of a pattern, before it starts to repeat, is called the period. When you find the period of a pattern, it is easy to extend the diagram for the next seconds or minutes or even hours.

Mathematics Example 1.1

Which of the following could be the period of the pattern of this lighthouse?

A. 2 seconds.
B. 3 seconds.
C. 5 seconds.
D. 12 seconds

Scoring and comments on Mathematics Example 1.1

Full Credit

Code 1: Response C: 5 seconds.

No Credit

Code 0: Other responses.

Item type: Multiple-choice
Competency cluster: Connections
Overarching idea: Change and relationships
Situation: Public

The unusual way this authentic problem is presented to the students immediately moves it beyond the *reproduction* competency cluster. The graphical representation will be new to most, if not all, students. This involves interpretation and reasoning skills right from the start of the problem. Most students will probably simulate the situation mentally: dark-dark-light-dark-light-dark-dark-light- and so on. They will have to find the "rhythm", either with the help of the graphical representation or with some other representation like the more word-oriented one just presented. This activity of making connections between different representations does make the problem fit into *connections* competency cluster.

The underlying concept of periodicity is important not only within the discipline of mathematics but also in daily life. The field trial suggests that most students do not find this problem very difficult, in spite of its unfamiliar appearance.

Some might argue that the context could favour students living near the sea or an ocean. It should be pointed out however that mathematical literacy includes the ability to use mathematics in contexts different from the local one. That does not necessarily mean that students living close to the sea might not be in a somewhat advantaged position. However, the item by country analysis gives no indication that this is the case here: landlocked countries did not perform differently from countries bordering on oceans.

Mathematics Example 1.2

For how many seconds does the lighthouse send out light flashes in 1 minute?

A. 4
B. 12
C. 20
D. 24

Scoring and comments on Mathematics Example 1.2

Full Credit

Code 1: Response D: 24.

No Credit

Code 0: Other responses.

Item type: Multiple-choice
Competency cluster: Connections
Overarching idea: Change and relationships
Situation: Public

....

This example is slightly more difficult than Example 1.1, and the problem is also somewhat different in nature. The students have to translate and extend the visual model provided to a numeric model that helps them analyse the periodic pattern over a minute. It is not necessary that students have answered Example 1.1 correctly, but using that result is one possible strategy: since the period is 5, there are 12 periods in a minute, and since each period has 2 light flashes; the answer must be 24.

Another strategy that students at this level can use is to look at the graph for either the first 10 or the first 12 seconds, since these are numbers by which you can divide 60. If they look at 10 seconds, they will see 4 light flashes, to be multiplied by 6, and indeed the answer will again be 24. However, we do not really have "proof" that they fully understood the problem. The same holds for 12 seconds: 4 light flashes times 5 will give the students 20, which is wrong. The difference is that by choosing 10, the students have exactly 2 periods, and by choosing 12, they do not have a multiple of the period.

An authentic problem, not too difficult, associated with the *connections* cluster also because of the multiple steps needed.

Mathematics Example 1.3

In the diagram below, make a graph of a possible pattern of light flashes of a lighthouse that sends out light flashes for 30 seconds per minute. The period of this pattern must be equal to 6 seconds.

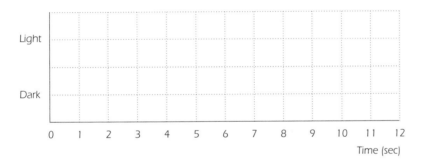

Scoring and comments on Mathematics Example 1.3

Full Credit

Code 2: Answers in which the graph shows a pattern of light and dark with flashes for 3 seconds in every 6 seconds, and with a period of 6 seconds. This can be done in the following ways:

- 1 one-second flash and 1 two-second flash (and this can be shown in several ways), or

- 1 three-second flash (which can be shown in four different ways).

- If 2 periods are shown, the pattern must be identical for each period.

Partial Credit

Code 1: Answers in which the graph shows a pattern of light and dark with flashes for 3 seconds in every 6 seconds, but the period is not 6 seconds. If 2 periods are shown, the pattern must be identical for each period.

- 3 one-second flashes, alternating with 3 one-second dark periods.

No Credit

Code 0: Other answers.

Item type: Open constructed-response
Competency cluster: Reflection
Overarching idea: Change and relationships
Situation: Public

....

The wording of the problem already indicates how "open" the problem is: "make a graph of a *possible* pattern of light flashes". Although the question seems to be related rather closely to the previous two questions, the correct response rate of the students was considerably lower, which made this item "rather difficult".

It is interesting that students are actually requested to "construct" or "design" something, which seems an important aspect of mathematical literacy: using mathematical competencies not only in a passive or derived way, but constructing an answer. Solving the problem is not trivial, because there are two conditions to be satisfied: equal amounts of time light and dark ("30 seconds per minute"), and a period of six seconds. This combination makes it essential that students really get at the conceptual level of understanding periodicity – already an indication that we are dealing with the *reflection* competency cluster.

Mathematics Unit 2
POSTAL CHARGES

The postal charges in Zedland are based on the weight of the items (to the nearest gram), as shown in the table below:

Weight (to nearest gram)	Charge
Up to 20 g	0.46 zeds
21 g – 50 g	0.69 zeds
51 g – 100 g	1.02 zeds
101 g – 200 g	1.75 zeds
201 g – 350 g	2.13 zeds
351 g – 500 g	2.44 zeds
501 g – 1000 g	3.20 zeds
1001 g – 2000 g	4.27 zeds
2001 g – 3000 g	5.03 zeds

Mathematics Example 2.1

Which one of the following graphs is the best representation of the postal charges in Zedland?
(The horizontal axis shows the weight in grams, and the vertical axis shows the charge in zeds.)

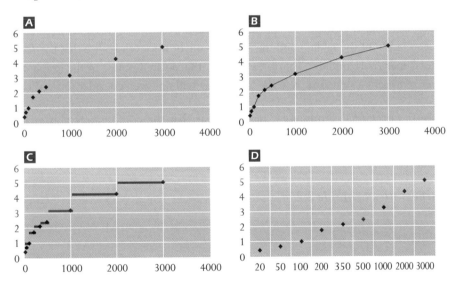

Scoring and comments on Mathematics Example 2.1

Full Credit

Code 1: Response C

No Credit

Code 0: Other responses.

Item type: Multiple-choice
Competency cluster: Connections
Overarching idea: Uncertainty
Situation: Public

The situation is clearly public and the problem is encountered frequently, but not necessarily in this form. In daily life citizens just hand in the postal package and ask what the postal charge will be. But informed citizens are expected to reflect a bit on the structure of the postal charges system and similar structures. Many people would know that the increase in postal charges is initially rather steep, but that with more weight, the increases get smaller. This structure is a rather common one.

To realise that such a structure can be made visual is quite another aspect. The graph is a "step graph", which students rarely, if at all, encounter in their school curriculum. This is probably the main reason why students found this problem quite difficult. Students are trained to connect the points in graphs, and sometimes they are wondering whether to connect the points with straight lines or with a nice curve – just like alternative B in the first example. B indeed seems to be a good answer, as it gives a price for every weight, unlike alternative A. The problem of course is that not all prices "exist", and that the range of prices is very limited: 0.46-0.69-1.02 and so on. Graph B is therefore incorrect. Graph C best fits the table of weights and charges as presented.

Another complicating factor in linking the table to a graph is the fact that graphs belonging to alternatives A, B and C all are very difficult to read for the first 500 grams because of the scales used. If students are really interested in the lowest values, alternative D might be appealing to them because it gives a very readable interpretation of the table – and the students might not even realise that the scale is not linear (horizontally). But if they realise the isolated points of the graph can never represent a structure as in the table, they will not even consider this option.

From the previous comments it may be clear that the competency cluster has to be *connections*, because of the unusual representation and the interpretation skills required to solve it.

Mathematics Example 2.2

Jan wants to send two items, weighing 40 grams and 80 grams respectively, to a friend.

According to the postal charges in Zedland, decide whether it is cheaper to send the two items as one parcel, or send the items as two separate parcels. Show your calculations of the cost in each case.

Scoring and comments on Mathematics Example 2.2

Full Credit

Code 1: Answers which specify that it will be cheaper to send the items as two separate parcels. The cost will be 1.71 zeds for two separate parcels, and 1.75 zeds for one single parcel containing both items.

No Credit

Code 0: Other answers.

Item type: Open constructed-response
Competency cluster: Connections
Overarching idea: Quantity
Situation: Public

This example is more practical than the previous one and was found to be relatively easy by the students during the field trial.

The example should be classified as belonging to the *connections* cluster, as the problem is not familiar to the students and requires just a bit more than reproduction competencies. Jan wants to send two items, 40 g and 80 g, to a friend. Although a bit counter-intuitive, the answer is easily found in the tables: 40 g cost 0.69 zeds, 80 g cost 1.02 zeds, so two parcels cost 1.71 zeds. One parcel weighing 120 g would cost 1.75 zeds to send. This is not mathematically complex, but is a relevant example of mathematical literacy, the kind of question that occurs in different situations in a citizen's life.

Mathematics Unit 3
HEARTBEAT

> For health reasons people should limit their efforts, for instance during sports, in order not to exceed a certain heartbeat frequency.
>
> For years the relationship between a person s recommended maximum heart rate and the person's age was described by the following formula:
>
> **Recommended maximum heart rate = 220 – age**
>
> Recent research showed that this formula should be modified slightly. The new formula is as follows:
>
> **Recommended maximum heart rate = 208 – (0.7 x age)**

Mathematics Example 3.1

A newspaper article stated: "A result of using the new formula instead of the old one is that the recommended maximum number of heartbeats per minute for young people decreases slightly and for old people it increases slightly."

From which age onwards does the recommended maximum heart rate increase as a result of the introduction of the new formula? Show your work.

Scoring and comments on Mathematics Example 3.1

Full Credit

Code 1: Answers which specify 41 or 40.

> $220 - age = 208 - 0.7 \times age$ results in $age = 40$, so people above 40 will have a higher recommended maximum heart rate under the new formula.

No Credit

Code 0: Other answers.

Item type: Open constructed-response
Competency cluster: Connections
Overarching idea: Change and relationships
Situation: Public / Personal

....

The classification of the situation depends of course on whether or not people are actually interested in data about their own health and body. One can safely argue that this item is somewhat scientific (because of the use of formulas) but many sportsmen and women (joggers, bicyclists, rowers, walkers, etc.) really do measure their heartbeat quite regularly during their exercises. More and more inexpensive instruments using micro-technology have made this aspect of human wellbeing much more accessible to ordinary people. This explains the situation classification as "Public/Personal."

Because we are really dealing more with modelling and less with trivial problem solving, a classification to the *connections* cluster seems rather straightforward, as well as the overarching idea *change and relationships*.

Comparing two formulas, even though they are merely rules of thumb, that relate to a person's well-being can be an intriguing activity, especially as they are partly presented as "word" formulas. This usually makes them more accessible to students. Even without asking a question, an initial reaction of students might be to see how their own age will lead to different recommended outcomes. As the PISA students are 15 years of age, the result under the old formula is 205 heartbeats per minute (realising that the information that the rate is *per minute* is not given), and under the new formula it is 198 (or 197). Thus they might already have found an indication that the statement in the newspaper article seems to be correct.

The example posed is somewhat more complex than this. It requires the students to find out when (at which age) the two formulas give the same result. This can be done by trial and error (a well established strategy by many students) but the more algebraic way seems more likely: $220 - a = 208 - (0.7 \times a)$, leading to an answer around 40.

From the viewpoint of mathematical literacy as well as from the viewpoint of more curricular oriented mathematics, this is quite an interesting and relevant problem. We note that the field trial data indicate that 15-year-old students found this problem quite difficult.

Mathematics Example 3.2

The formula *recommended maximum heart rate* = 208 – (0.7 x *age*) is also used to determine when physical training is most effective. Research has shown that physical training is most effective when the heartbeat is at 80% of the recommended maximum heart rate.

Write down a formula for calculating the heart rate for most effective physical training, expressed in terms of age.

Scoring and comments on Mathematics Example 3.2

Full Credit

Code 1: Answers which present any formula that is the equivalent of multiplying the formula for recommended maximum heart rate by 80 per cent.

- heart rate $= 166 - 0.56 \times$ age.
- heart rate $= 166 - 0.6 \times$ age.
- h $= 166 - 0.56 \times$ a.
- h $= 166 - 0.6 \times$ a.
- heart rate $= (208 - 0.7 \times$ age$) \times 0.8$.

No Credit

Code 0: Other answers.

Item type: Open constructed-response
Competency cluster: Connections
Overarching idea: Change and relationships
Situation: Public / Personal

....

This example *seems* to measure exactly the same competencies as Example 3.1. The correct response rate is almost identical (during field trial). But there is a notable difference: in Example 3.1 students have to compare two formulas and to decide when they give the same result. In Example 3.2 the students are asked to "construct" a formula, something they are not frequently asked to do during their school career, in many countries. From a strictly mathematical viewpoint the question is not difficult at all: just multiply the formula by 0.8 – for instance, *Heart Rate = (208 – 0.7 × age) × 0.8*. It would seem that even such simple manipulation of algebraic expressions, expressed in a practical and realistic context, presents a substantial challenge to many 15-year-olds.

Mathematics Unit 4
PAYMENTS BY AREA

> People living in an apartment building decide to buy the building. They will put their money together in such a way that each will pay an amount that is proportional to the size of their apartment.
>
> For example, a man living in an apartment that occupies one fifth of the floor area of all apartments will pay one fifth of the total price of the building.

Mathematics Example 4.1

Circle Correct or Incorrect for each of the following statements.

Statement	Correct / Incorrect
A person living in the largest apartment will pay more money for each square metre of his apartment than the person living in the smallest apartment.	Correct / Incorrect
If we know the areas of two apartments and the price of one of them we can calculate the price of the second.	Correct / Incorrect
If we know the price of the building and how much each owner will pay, then the total area of all apartments can be calculated.	Correct / Incorrect
If the total price of the building were reduced by 10%, each of the owners would pay 10% less.	Correct / Incorrect

Scoring and comments on Mathematics Example 4.1

Full Credit

Code 1: Answers which specify: Incorrect, Correct, Incorrect, Correct, in this order.

No Credit

Code 0: Any other combination of answers.

Item type: Complex multiple-choice
Competency cluster: Connections
Overarching idea: Change and relationships
Situation: Public

....

The item demands quite a high level of competence in proportional reasoning, relating to a practical situation in society that is likely to be somewhat unfamiliar to 15-year-olds. The complex multiple-choice format used requires students to demonstrate a quite thorough understanding of the concepts involved. In addition, students are required to read and understand a series of complex mathematical propositions. The item was found to be quite difficult in the field trial.

Mathematics Example 4.2

There are three apartments in the building. The largest, apartment 1, has a total area of 95m². Apartments 2 and 3 have areas of 85m² and 70m² respectively. The selling price for the building is 300 000 zeds.

How much should the owner of apartment 2 pay? Show your work.

Scoring and comments on Mathematics Example 4.2

Full Credit

Code 2: Answers which specify 102 000 zeds, with or without the calculation shown. Unit not required.

- Apartment 2: 102 000 zeds

- Apt. 2: $\dfrac{85}{250}$ x 300 000 = 102 000 *zeds*

- $\dfrac{300\,000}{250}$ = 1200 zeds for each square metre, so apartment 2 is 102 000.

Partial Credit

Code 1: Answers in which students applied the correct method, but present minor computational errors.

- Apt. 2: $\dfrac{85}{250}$ x 300 000 = 10 200 *zeds*

No Credit

Code 0: Other answers.

Item type: Open constructed-response
Competency cluster: Connections
Overarching idea: Quantity
Situation: Public

....

Example 4.2 is a more concrete example, involving "real" apartments, with "real" areas. The field trial results confirm that this question is considerably easier than the more abstract first question.

The competency cluster classification *connections* is appropriate given the multi-step problem solving, in an unfamiliar context, that is needed.

Mathematics Unit 5
STUDENT HEIGHTS

Mathematics Example 5.1

In a mathematics class one day, the heights of all students were measured. The average height of boys was 160 cm, and the average height of girls was 150 cm. Alena was the tallest – her height was 180 cm. Zdenek was the shortest – his height was 130 cm.

Two students were absent from class that day, but they were in class the next day. Their heights were measured, and the averages were recalculated. Amazingly, the average height of the girls and the average height of the boys did not change.

Which of the following conclusions can be drawn from this information?

Circle "Yes" or "No" for each conclusion.

Conclusion	Can this conclusion be drawn?
Both students are girls.	Yes / No
One of the students is a boy and the other is a girl.	Yes / No
Both students have the same height.	Yes / No
The average height of all students did not change.	Yes / No
Zdenek is still the shortest.	Yes / No

Scoring and comments on Mathematics Example 5.1

Full Credit

Code 1: Answers which specify "No" for all conclusions.

No Credit

Code 0: Any other combination of answers.

Item type: Complex multiple-choice
Competency cluster: Reflection
Overarching idea: Uncertainty
Situation: Educational

....

The classification is rather straightforward: *uncertainty*, since it requires understanding of statistical concepts; *educational*, since it is the kind of problem that one would only come across in a school setting; and *reflection*, because of the rather heavy "communications" aspect – students have to really understand the language, in detail, and the underlying concepts, which are rather sophisticated as well. The problem involves the ability to pose questions ("how do I know…?", "how do I find…?", "what can happen?", "what would happen if…?"), and the ability to understand and handle mathematical concepts (average) in contexts that are complex.

The mathematisation aspect of identifying the relevant mathematical content and information is important in this example. Superficial reading will lead to a misinterpretation. The situation is indeed complex: it varies within the class, and over time The entity "class" is used while discussing the average for *boys* and average for *girls* independently, but subsequently it is stated that Alena is the tallest (girl or student) and Zdenek the shortest (boy or student). The students have to read carefully to notice that Zdenek is a boy, which is essential, and Alena is a girl. The variation over time is that two students are not present initially, but when included in the measurement the next day the averages remain unchanged. The class thus gets bigger, but you don't know whether the two extra students are girls, boys or one of each.

For students to get the five parts of this item correct, they need to explore in quite a sophisticated way the relationship between the data and the statistical summaries of those data. The field trial showed that this was an extremely challenging item for 15-year-olds.

Mathematics Unit 6
SWING

Mathematics Example 6.1

Mohammed is sitting on a swing. He starts to swing. He is trying to go as high as possible.

Which diagram best represents the height of his feet above the ground as he swings?

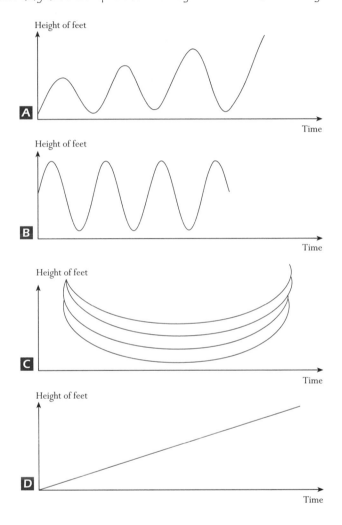

Scoring and comments on Mathematics Example 6.1

Full Credit

Code 1: Response A.

No Credit

Code 0: Other responses.

Item type: Multiple-choice
Competency cluster: Connections
Overarching idea: Change and relationships
Situation: Personal

This kind of item is rather popular in some countries: which graphical representation fits the short story? In the 1970s the Canadian math educator Janvier promoted the format by asking students to identify a race track that would fit with the speed graph given – so more or less the other way around. A similar item was used in PISA 2000 and can be found in the publication *Sample Tasks from the PISA 2000 Assessment* (OECD, Paris, 2002a).

In the case of the swing, the question seems easier than the PISA 2000 item because one can easily dismiss certain alternatives almost immediately, which was certainly not the case with the race track problem.

Answer A seems to fit rather nicely. B does not start with feet low and does not get higher with each swing, C is just a visualisation of the swing action, and D does not swing. Answer A is therefore the most likely, which a majority of the students agree with.

The classification *connections* is appropriate since the students have to interpret and link at least two representations, textual and graphic, and link the best graph to the text. The familiarity of the context may bring a further practical component to the evaluation of the response options. Students have to understand the graph within the familiar context presented, but the graphic representations are not so familiar.

Mathematics Unit 7
WATER TANK

Mathematics Example 7.1

A water tank has shape and dimensions as shown in the diagram.

At the beginning the tank is empty. Then it is filled with water at the rate of one litre per second.

Which of the following graphs shows how the height of the water surface changes over time?

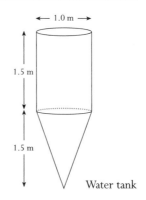

Water tank

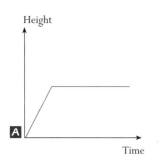

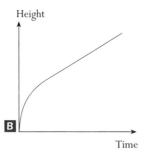

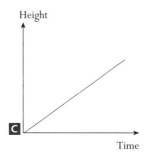

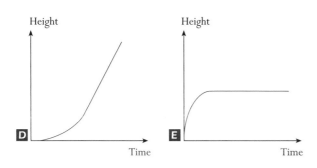

Scoring and comments on Mathematics Example 7.1

Full Credit

Code 1: Response B.

No Credit

Code 0: Other responses.

Item type: Multiple-choice
Competency cluster: Connections
Overarching idea: Change and relationships
Situation: Scientific

This example is not very complex for students to understand: there is very little text and a clear diagram. Students are required to link the text and diagram, and then relate their understanding to graphical representations. These competencies fall into the *connections* cluster.

It is interesting to see that this item actually has quite a bit of redundant information. The measures of the tank are detailed, and the constant rate is described as one litre per second. But all this quantification does not help the students, since the graphs are "global" or "qualitative" only. This is interesting because one does not often see redundant information in mathematical items, but redundancy occurs almost every time one deals with problems in the real world. Actually, an important part of any mathematisation process is to identify the relevant mathematics and get rid of the redundant information.

Although the item is classified as having a scientific context, similar problems occur in personal situations. Filling a glass or vase or bucket, especially when the container is not cylindrical in shape, can cause some surprises if one does not take into account how the speed of the increase in height depends on the shape of the container, and such awareness fits under the definition of mathematical literacy.

Mathematics Unit 8
REACTION TIME

In a sprinting event, the "reaction time" is the time interval between the starter's gun firing and the athlete leaving the starting block. The "final time" includes both this reaction time, and the running time.

The following table gives the reaction time and the final time of 8 runners in a 100 metre sprint race.

Lane	Reaction time (sec)	Final time (sec)
1	0.147	10.09
2	0.136	9.99
3	0.197	9.87
4	0.180	Did not finish the race
5	0.210	10.17
6	0.216	10.04
7	0.174	10.08
8	0.193	10.13

Mathematics Example 8.1

Identify the Gold, Silver and Bronze medallists from this race. Fill in the table below with the medallists' lane number, reaction time and final time.

Medal	Lane	Reaction time (sec)	Final time (sec)
Gold			
Silver			
Bronze			

Scoring and comments on Mathematics Example 8.1

Full Credit

Code 1:

Medal	Lane	Reaction time (sec)	Final time (sec)
Gold	3	0.197	9.87
Silver	2	0.136	9.99
Bronze	6	0.216	10.04

No Credit

Code 0: Other answers.

Item type: Open constructed-response
Competency cluster: Reproduction
Overarching idea: Quantity
Situation: Scientific

....

A *reproduction* item that deals with understanding decimal notation (Quantity) but with some redundancy and complexity added because of the reaction time, which is not necessary to answer the first example. Almost two-thirds of the students that participated in the field trial came up with the correct answer, indicating that it is a relatively easy item for most 15-year-olds.

Mathematics Example 8.2

To date, no humans have been able to react to a starter's gun in less than 0.110 second.

If the recorded reaction time for a runner is less than 0.110 second, then a false start is considered to have occurred because the runner must have left before hearing the gun.

If the Bronze medallist had a faster reaction time, would he have had a chance to win the Silver medal? Give an explanation to support your answer.

Scoring and comments on Mathematics Example 8.2

Full Credit

Code 1: Answers which specify "yes", with an adequate explanation. For example:

- Yes. If he had a reaction time 0.05 sec faster, he would have equalled second place.

- Yes, he would have a chance to win the Silver medal if his reaction time were less than or equal to 0.166 sec.

- Yes, with the fastest possible reaction time he would have done a 9.93, which is good enough for the Silver medal.

No Credit

Code 0: Other answers, including answers which specify "yes" without an adequate explanation.

Item type: Open constructed-response
Competency cluster: Connections
Overarching idea: Quantity
Situation: Scientific

This example requires a moderate degree of verbal reasoning as well as mathematical reasoning. If one has answered Example 8.1 correctly, one sees clearly that Lane 6 (Bronze) is a slow starter (actually the slowest of all) and Lane 2 (Silver) a very fast starter (the fastest of them all), but they ended up with almost the same final time (different by only 0.05 seconds). The Lane 6 runner could thus have grabbed the Silver medal had his reaction been a bit faster, since the difference in their reaction times was quite a bit greater than the difference in final times.

Because of the interpretation skills needed, and the less trivial comparison of decimal numbers with different degrees of rounding, this item fits the *connections* competency cluster.

Mathematics Unit 9
BUILDING BLOCKS

Susan likes to build blocks from small cubes like the one shown in the following diagram:

Small cube

Susan has lots of small cubes like this one. She uses glue to join cubes together to make other blocks.

First, Susan glues eight of the cubes together to make the block shown in Diagram A:

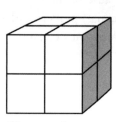

Diagram A

Then Susan makes the solid blocks shown in Diagram B and Diagram C below:

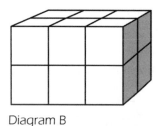

Diagram B   Diagram C

Mathematics Example 9.1

How many small cubes will Susan need to make the block shown in Diagram B?

Answer: _____ cubes.

Scoring and comments on Mathematics Example 9.1

Full Credit

Code 1: Answers which specify 12 cubes.

No Credit

Code 0: Other answers.

Item type: Open constructed-response
Competency cluster: Reproduction
Overarching idea: Space and shape
Situation: Personal

In every item bank it is compulsory to have really easy items as well as more difficult ones, as measured by students' results. This question is easy indeed: the students can imagine the problem easily, as they have probably been using these kinds of blocks often (Duplo, Lego, etc) and do not even need multiplication to get to the correct answer. For diagram B they see the first six cubes, and they know there are six cubes at the back. Both the familiarity as well as the simplicity makes this a clear *reproduction* item.

Mathematics Example 9.2

How many small cubes will Susan need to make the solid block shown in Diagram C?

Answer: _____ cubes.

Scoring and comments on Mathematics Example 9.2

Full Credit

Code 1: Answers which specify 27 cubes.

No Credit

Code 0: Other answers.

Item type: Open constructed-response
Competency cluster: Reproduction
Overarching idea: Space and shape
Situation: Personal

....

Example 9.2 differs from Example 9.1 in that the number of cubes is somewhat higher (27 instead of 12), but conceptually it is the same question. Field trial data show that students found this item relatively easy. This is to be expected because of the very basic competencies needed to solve this problem. Experts from participating countries also agreed that items such as this are close to their respective curricula.

Mathematics Example 9.3

Susan realises that she used more small cubes than she really needed to make a block like the one shown in Diagram C. She realises that she could have glued small cubes together to look like Diagram C, but the block could have been hollow on the inside.

What is the minimum number of cubes she needs to make a block that looks like the one shown in Diagram C, but is hollow?

Answer: _____ cubes.

Scoring and comments on Mathematics Example 9.3

Full Credit

Code 1: Answers which specify 26 cubes.

No Credit

Code 0: Other answers.

Item type: Open constructed-response
Competency cluster: Connections
Overarching idea: Space and shape
Situation: Personal

....

In Example 9.2 the assumption was that we were working with loose cubes and therefore needed 27, otherwise the block would collapse. If we are allowed to use glue, it may be possible to construct a block as depicted in C, but using fewer than 27 blocks. Although the "obvious" answer is 26 (take out the centre cube), more can be observed about this example. The problem is that the question does not explicitly state that Block C must look the same from all directions. This is relevant because one can take out more than one cube if one is allowed to use glue and has to stick to diagram C. However, it is *implicitly* stated by saying that the block has to be hollow on the *inside,* which takes care of this problem. From a language and interpretation point of view, however, this is not a straightforward question.

It can be classified as belonging to the *connections* cluster for several reasons: the mathematisation required to grasp the essentials of the question, the need to interpret Diagram C mentally as if it had a hole in it, the reasoning and thinking involved in order to reach the correct answer, and the lack of a standard procedure or algorithm.

Mathematics Example 9.4

Now Susan wants to make a block that looks like a solid block that is 6 small cubes long, 5 small cubes wide and 4 small cubes high. She wants to use the smallest number of cubes possible, by leaving the largest possible hollow space inside the block.

What is the minimum number of cubes Susan will need to make this block?

Answer: _____ cubes.

Scoring and comments on Mathematics Example 9.4

Full Credit

Code 1: Answers which specify 96 cubes.

No Credit

Code 0: Other answers.

Item type: Open-Constructed Response
Competency cluster: Reflection
Overarching idea: Space and shape
Situation: Personal

In Example 9.4 we need to assume (because of the way the problem is stated) that we can use glue again. The problem is now: "what is the minimum number of cubes necessary to build a hollow 4 x 5 x 6 block?"

As noted before, there are no standard problem- solving heuristics available to the students to answer this question. Having a mental image of one missing cube within a 3 x 3 x 3 building is quite another matter. Instead of having to mentally remove one cube, the students need to come up with a more generalisable strategy, involving more mathematical reasoning. It therefore makes sense to classify this item as belonging to the *reflection* competency cluster.

How can students find the right answer? A good strategy would be to start with the maximum number of cubes: 6 x 5 x 4 makes 120 altogether. Then mentally take out as many as possible from the centre. As it is 6 long, you can take out 4; as it is 5 wide, you can take out 3; as it is 4 high, you can take out 2. The total is 4 x 3 x 2, which equals 24. That gives 120-24 = 96, which is correct. It is a nice strategy, showing some real understanding. In a classroom situation, it might be interesting to ask the students for an explanation of their reasoning to discover useful teaching techniques.

Another strategy would be to look at the walls that are necessary to get the desired block. A picture might be helpful in this case.

To build the front wall we need 5 x 4 cubes; for the back wall, another 5 x 4 cubes. For the side wall we do not need 6 x 4 because we have already the front and back covered. The length of the side walls is therefore not 6 but 4, requiring 4 x 4 for each side. Finally we need to cover the bottom and top, leaving out what we have already. This gives us another 3 x 4. Total: 5 x 4; 5 x 4; 4 x 4; 4 x 4; 3 x 4; 3 x 4 – altogether, 96.

Undoubtedly, students will have different strategies at hand. A study like PISA could sometimes be used to find out which strategies are created or used by students when dealing with such a complex problem, where one has limited ways of representation in the traditional sense.

This is quite a challenging problem, almost strictly intra-mathematic, but still requiring competencies and skills, such as spatial visualisation, that are vital for literacy in mathematics.

Mathematics Unit 10
DRUG CONCENTRATIONS

Mathematics Example 10.1

A woman in hospital receives an injection of penicillin. Her body gradually breaks the penicillin down so that one hour after the injection only 60% of the penicillin will remain active.

This pattern continues: at the end of each hour only 60% of the penicillin that was present at the end of the previous hour remains active.

Suppose the woman is given a dose of 300 milligrams of penicillin at 8 o'clock in the morning.

Complete this table showing the amount of penicillin that will remain active in the woman's blood at intervals of one hour from 0800 until 1100 hours.

Time	0800	0900	1000	1100
Penicillin (mg)	300			

Scoring and comments on Mathematics Example 10.1

Full Credit

Code 2: Answers which include all three correct table entries, such as:

Time	0800	0900	1000	1100
Penicillin (mg)	300	180	108	64.8 or 65

Partial Credit

Code 1: Answers which include one or two correct table entries.

No Credit

Code 0: Other answers.

Item type: Open constructed-response
Competency cluster: Connections
Overarching idea: Change and relationships
Situation: Scientific

....

This first example may seem rather uncomplicated but exponential decay is not a trivial matter to many students. 60% of 60% of 60% of... may look like a simple rule but results on items like this one show that this is not the case. Although percentages are treated quite extensively in primary school, students are often not prepared to operationalise this knowledge in a different situation. To identify the relevant mathematical information means understanding the

percentual or exponential decay (not necessarily understanding the expressions as such, but the concept), identifying the start-value (300) and applying the process repeatedly.

It is interesting that so many of the students tested in the field trial (50 per cent) failed to find the correct answer. This is important information for judging the quality and/or effectiveness of the teaching/learning process.

Mathematics Example 10.2

Peter has to take 80 mg of a drug to control his blood pressure. The following graph shows the initial amount of the drug, and the amount that remains active in Peter's blood after one, two, three and four days.

Amount of active drug (mg)

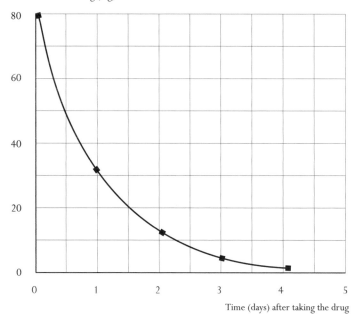

Time (days) after taking the drug

How much of the drug remains active at the end of the first day?

A. 6 mg.

B. 12 mg.

C. 26 mg.

D. 32 mg.

Scoring and comments on Mathematics Example 10.2

Full Credit

Code 1: Response D: 32 mg.

No Credit

Code 0: Other responses.

Item type: *Multiple-choice*
Competency cluster: *Reproduction*
Overarching idea: *Change and relationships*
Situation: *Scientific*

....

This example is easier than the previous one and actually requires nothing more than reading a graph, which leads to the conclusion that the item would require *reproduction* competencies. However, the item is set in a somewhat unusual context and some interpretation is needed.

Mathematics Example 10.3

From the graph for the previous question it can be seen that each day, about the same proportion of the previous day's drug remains active in Peter's blood.

At the end of each day which of the following is the approximate percentage of the previous day's drug that remains active?

A. 20%.

B. 30%.

C. 40%.

D. 80%.

Scoring and comments on Mathematics Example 10.3

Full Credit

Code 1: Response C: 40%.

No Credit

Code 0: Other responses.

Item type: *Multiple-choice*
Competency cluster: *Connections*
Overarching idea: *Change and relationships*
Situation: *Scientific*

....

Example 10.3 relates to the graph presented with Example 10.2. The question is "what is the rate of decay?" in this particular situation. Presenting this question in multiple-choice format lets the students make an educated guess because they know the starting value, 80, and the next value – 32 (if they had answered Example 10.2 correctly) or around 30 (if they ignore Example 10.2 and go directly to the graph), and 3/8 is quite close to 40 per cent. The interpretation demands of the question places this item in the *connections* competency cluster.

Mathematics Unit 11
TWISTED BUILDING

In modern architecture, buildings often have unusual shapes. The picture below shows a computer model of a "twisted building" and a plan of the ground floor.

The compass points show the orientation of the building.

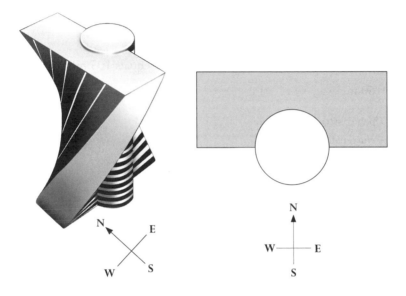

The ground floor of the building contains the main entrance and has room for shops. Above the ground floor there are 20 storeys containing apartments.

The plan of each storey is similar to the plan of the ground floor, but each has a slightly different orientation from the storey below. The cylinder contains the elevator shaft and a landing on each floor.

Mathematics Example 11.1

Estimate the total height of the building, in metres. Explain how you found your answer.

Scoring and comments on Mathematics Example 11.1

Full Credit

Code 2: Answers ranging from 50 to 90 metres, accompanied by a correct explanation. For example:

- One floor of the building has a height of about 2.5 meters. There is some extra room between floors. Therefore an estimate is 21 x 3 = 63 metres.

- Allow 4 m for each story. 20 of these equals 80 m, plus 10 m for the ground floor, which gives a total of 90 m.

Partial Credit

Code 1: Answers which present the correct calculation method and explanation, but using 20 stories instead of 21. For example:

- Each apartment could be 3.5 metres high; 20 stories of 3.5 metres gives a total height of 70 m.

No Credit

Code 0: Other answers, including answers without any explanation, answers with other incorrect numbers of floors, and answers with unreasonable estimates of the height of each floor (4 m would be the upper limit). For example:

- Each floor is around 5 m high, so 5 x 21 equals 105 metres.

- 60 m.

Item type: Open constructed-response
Competency cluster: Connections
Overarching idea: Space and shape
Situation: Public

....

The items in this unit require some imagination and insight, particularly in the area of spatial visualisation, in a public context that has familiar elements, but may seem novel to many students. The first example asks students to make some sensible judgments about what might be a reasonable height for each storey of a multi-storey building, including both the "visible" height of rooms in each storey and an allowance for the space needed between floors. Students need to carry out some elementary modelling, and to translate a visual representation into a numeric representation. These competencies are associated with the *connections* cluster.

Many students in the field trial were able to do this, with the item slightly favouring boys. However, the item had a high omission rate, indicating that a good number of students were unwilling or unable to use their imagination in the required way.

Mathematics Example 11.2

The following pictures are sideviews of the twisted building.

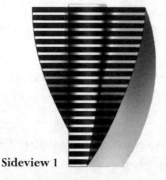

Sideview 1   **Sideview 2**

From which direction has Sideview 1 been drawn?

A. From the North.

B. From the West.

C. From the East.

D. From the South.

Scoring and comments on Mathematics Example 11.2

Full Credit

Code 1: Response C: From the East.

No Credit

Code 0: Other responses.

Item type: Multiple-choice
Competency cluster: Connections
Overarching idea: Space and shape
Situation: Public

The second example asks students to mentally compare different visual representations of a building, and to choose from options that could describe the relationship between those representations. The spatial reasoning involved places the item in the *connections* cluster.

This item was considerably easier than the first one, but showed poor measurement properties in a number of participating countries. It may be that the quality of the graphic used in the field trial version was inadequate for the high visual demands of the item.

Mathematics Example 11.3

From which direction has Sideview 2 been drawn?

A. From the North West.

B. From the North East.

C. From the South West.

D. From the South East.

Scoring and comments on Mathematics Example 11.3

Full Credit

Code 1: Response D: From the South East.

No Credit

Code 0: Other responses.

Item type: Multiple-choice
Competency cluster: Connections
Overarching idea: Space and shape
Situation: Public

....

The third example is very similar to Example 11.2. It is interesting to note the different visual cues provided by the two "sideviews" used as stimuli for Examples 11.2 and 11.3 respectively. Example 11.3 was a little more difficult than Example 11.2, possibly because of the subtlety of the shadows in the stimulus, and the interpretation demands they impose.

Mathematics Example 11.4

Each storey containing apartments has a certain "twist" compared to the ground floor. The top floor (the 20th floor above the ground floor) is at right angles to the ground floor.

The drawing below represents the ground floor.

Draw in this diagram the plan of the 10th floor above the ground floor, showing how this floor is situated compared to the ground floor.

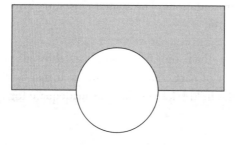

Scoring and comments on Mathematics Example 11.4

Full Credit

Code 2: Answers which present a correct drawing, meaning correct rotation point and anti-clockwise rotation. Accept angles from 40° to 50°.

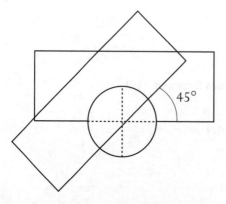

Partial Credit

Code 1: Answers which incorrectly present either the rotation angle, the rotation point, or the rotation direction incorrect.

No Credit

Code 0: Other answers.

Item type: Open constructed-response
Competency cluster: Connections
Overarching idea: Space and shape
Situation: Public

....

The fourth example asks students to imagine the cumulative effect of the twisting phenomenon over a number of steps, and to construct a graphic representation of the 10th floor. Again the spatial reasoning involved places this item in the *connections* cluster of competencies.

This item is relatively difficult, and again had quite a high omission rate in the field trial. It would seem that many 15-year-old students find this kind of geometric construction quite challenging.

Mathematics unit 12
ROCK CONCERT

Mathematics Example 12.1

For a rock concert a rectangular field of size 100 m by 50 m was reserved for the audience. The concert was completely sold out and the field was full with all the fans standing.

Which one of the following is likely to be the best estimate of the total number of people attending the concert?

A. 2 000

B. 5 000

C. 20 000

D. 50 000

E. 100 000

Scoring and comments on Mathematics Example 12.1

Full Credit

Code 1: Response C: 20 000.

No Credit

Code 0: Other responses.

Item type: Multiple-choice
Competency cluster: Connections
Overarching idea: Quantity
Situation: Public

The mathematics framework highlights the importance of estimation skills as a part of the quantitative armoury of the mathematically literate citizen. This item is placed in a context that should be reasonably familiar to many 15-year-old students. However, after a small amount of interpretation, it requires students to take an active role in making assumptions about how much space (on average) people standing in a crowd might reasonably occupy. The kind of problem posing, and the mathematical reasoning it implies, places the item in the *connections* cluster.

Five response options were provided, so students had only to select the best option. Option A (2 000) implies that people would occupy on average 2.5 square meters, hardly a crowded concert. Option E (100 000) implies that on average there would be 20 people per square meter, barely possible and certainly not realistic. That leaves students to decide between three intermediate densities: 1 person, 4 people or 10 people per square meter. Which is more realistic under the conditions described (completely sold out, and the field was full with all the fans standing)? About 30 per cent of students in the field trial chose the most reasonable middle option C (20 000).

Mathematics Unit 13
MOVING WALKWAYS

Mathematics Example 13.1

On the right is a photograph of moving walkways.

The following Distance-Time graph shows a comparison between "walking on the moving walkway" and "walking on the ground next to the moving walkway."

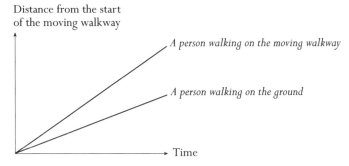

Assuming that, in the above graph, the walking pace is about the same for both persons, add a line to the graph that would represent the distance versus time for a person who is standing still on the moving walkway.

Scoring and comments on Mathematics Example 13.1

Full Credit

Code 1: Answers which show a line below the two lines, but it must be closer to the line of "a person walking on the ground" than to the baseline.

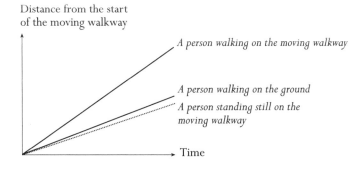

No Credit

Code 0: Other answers.

Item type: Open constructed-response
Competency cluster: Reflection
Overarching idea: Change and relationships
Situation: Scientific

The stimulus for this question depicts an object seen in some public places, and is also reminiscent of other similar phenomena that many 15-year-old students may be more familiar with (such as walking alongside a moving escalator, or running down stairs next to an elevator). However the nature of the question places this item in a "scientific" situation.

Students have to deal with a mathematical representation of the situation depicted, and must apply considerable imagination and insight to understand the representation. Quite sophisticated mathematical reasoning is then required to solve the problem and construct the appropriate response. These competencies are typical of the *reflection* cluster.

The item was found to be quite difficult by students in the field trial, with success rates around 15 per cent.

ELABORATION OF THE OVERARCHING IDEAS

Quantity

Description

In order to organise the world in which we live, there is a strong need for quantification: to express what is "big" or "small", "tall" or "short", "few" or "many", "more" or "less". We recognise patterns in the world around us while quantifying them: we call "fiveness" what collections of five apples, five people, five cars, five items have in common. The counting numbers 1, 2, 3, ...are a way of capturing and describing those patterns. The counting numbers provide a starting point for calculating activities and a source for the search for deeper patterns like even and odd.

But the counting numbers might not be the earliest phenomenological encounter for young children. Children can recognise "small" and "big" in a qualitative way without attaching numbers to them, both with objects of different sizes (big biscuit vs. small biscuit) and with collections of objects (three objects vs. seven objects).

If a magnitude is measured, we see a further number use that is most important in everyday life. Length, area, volume, height, speed, mass, air pressure, money value are all quantified using measures.

Quantitative reasoning is an important aspect of dealing with quantities. It includes:
- number sense;
- understanding the meaning of operations;
- having a feel for the magnitude of numbers;
- elegant computations;
- mental arithmetic;
- estimations.

The "meaning of operations" includes the ability to perform operations involving comparisons, ratios and percentages. Number sense addresses issues of relative size, different representations of numbers, equivalent form of numbers, and using understanding of these things to describe attributes of the world.

Quantity also includes having a "feeling" for quantities and estimation. In order to be able to test numerical results for reasonableness, one needs a broad knowledge of quantities (measures) in the real world. Is the average speed of a car 5, 50 or 500 km/h? Is the population of the world 6 million, 600 million, 6 billion, or 60 billion? How tall is a tower? How wide is a river? The ability to make quick order-of-magnitude approximations is of particular importance, especially when viewed in light of the increasing use of electronic calculating tools. One needs to be able to see that 33 X 613 is something around 20 000. To achieve this skill one does not need extensive training in mental execution of traditional written algorithms, but a flexible and smart application of place value understanding and single-digit arithmetic (Fey, 1990).

Using number sense in an appropriate way, students can solve problems requiring direct, inverse, and joint proportional reasoning. They are able to estimate rates of change and provide a rationale for the selection of data and level of precision required by operations and models they use. They can examine alternative algorithms, showing why they work or in what cases they fail. They can develop models involving operations, and relationships between operations, for problems involving real-world data and numerical relations requiring operations and comparisons (Dossey, 1997).

In the overarching idea *quantity*, there is a place for "elegant" quantitative reasoning like that used by Gauss, as discussed in the following example. Creativity coupled with conceptual understanding should be valued at the level of schooling that includes 15-year-olds.

Examples

Gauss

Karl Friedrich Gauss's (1777-1855) teacher had asked the class to add together all the numbers from 1 to 100. Presumably the teacher's aim was to keep the students occupied for a time. But Gauss was an excellent quantitative reasoner and spotted a shortcut to the solution. His reasoning went like this:

You write down the sum twice, once in ascending order, then in descending order, like this:

1 + 2 + 3 + ... + 98 + 99 + 100
100 + 99 + 98 +............+ 3 + 2 + 1

Now you add the two sums, column by column, to give:
101 + 101 +...................+ 101 + 101

As there are exactly 100 copies of the number 101 in this sum its value is
100 × 101 = 10 100.

Since this product is twice the answer to the original sum, if you halve it, you obtain the answer: 5 050.

Triangular numbers

We might elaborate this example of quantitative thinking involving patterns of numbers a little further to demonstrate a link with a geometric representation of that pattern, by showing the formula that gives the general situation for Gauss's problem:

$$1 + 2 + 3 + ... + n = n(n + 1)/2$$

This formula also captures a geometric pattern that is well known: numbers of the form n(n+1)/2 are called triangular numbers, since they are exactly the numbers that are obtained by arranging balls in an equilateral triangle.

The first five triangular numbers 1, 3, 6, 10, 15 are shown below in Figure 1.5:

Figure 1.5 ■ **The first five triangular numbers**

Proportional reasoning

It will be interesting to see how students in different countries solve problems that lend themselves to the use of a variety of strategies. Differences can be expected especially in the area of proportional reasoning. In certain countries, mainly one strategy per item is likely to be used, while in other countries more strategies will be used. Also, similarities in reasoning will appear in solving problems that do not look very similar. This is in line with recent research results on TIMSS data (Mitchell, J. *et al.*, 2000). The following three items illustrate this point about different strategies and the relationships among them:

1. *Tonight you're giving a party. You want to buy 100 cans of soft drink. How many six-can packs are you going to buy?*

2. *A hang-glider with glide-ratio 1 to 22 starts from a sheer cliff at 120 metres. The pilot is aiming at a spot at a distance of 1 400 metres. Will she reach that spot (under conditions of no wind)?*

3. *A school wants to rent mini-vans (with seats for eight passengers) for going to a school camp and 98 students need transportation. How many vans does the school need?*

The first problem could be seen as a division problem ($100 \div 6 =$ ___) that then leaves the student with an interpretation problem back to the context (what is the meaning of the remainder?). The second problem can be solved by proportional reasoning (for every metre height I can fly a distance of 22 metres, so starting from 120 metres...). The third problem will be solved by many as a division problem. All three problems, however, can be solved using the ratio table method:

Bottles :	1	10	5	15	2	17
	6	60	30	90	12	102

Flying :	1	100	20	120
	22	2 200	440	2 640

Buses :	1	10	2	13
	8	80	16	104

Seeing this similarity is a skill that belongs to mathematical literacy: mathematically literate students do not need to look for the one available and appropriate tool or algorithm, but have available to them a wide array of strategies from which they can choose.

Percents

Carl went to a store to buy a jacket with a normal price of 50 zed that was on sale for 20% off. In Zedland there is a 5% sales tax. The clerk first added the 5% tax to the price of the jacket and then took 20% off. Carl protested: he wanted the clerk to deduct the 20% discount first and then calculate the 5% tax.

Does it make any difference?

Problems involving this kind of quantitative thinking, and the need to carry out the resulting mental calculations, are encountered frequently when shopping. The ability to effectively handle such problems is fundamental to mathematical literacy.

Space and shape

Description

Shape is a vital, growing and fascinating thing in mathematics, with strong ties to traditional geometry but going far beyond it in content, meaning and method. Interaction with real shapes involves understanding the visual world around us, its description, and encoding and decoding of visual information. It also means interpretation of visual information. In order to grasp the concept of shapes, students should be able to discover the way in which objects are similar and how they differ, to analyse the different components of the object, and to recognise shapes in different dimensions and representations.

It is important not to restrict ourselves to shapes as static entities. A shape can be transformed as an entity, and shapes can be modified. These changes can sometimes be visualised very elegantly using computer technology. Students should be able to see the patterns and regularities when shapes are changing. An example is shown in Figure 1.6 in the following section.

Another important dynamic aspect of the study of shapes is the relative position of shapes to each other in relation to the position of an observer. To achieve this we must not only understand the relative position of objects, but also consider questions of how and why we see things this way, etc. The relationship between shapes or images and their representation in both two and three dimensions plays a key role here.

Examples requiring this kind of thinking are abundant. Identifying and relating a photograph of a city to a map of that city and indicating from which point a picture was taken; the ability to draw a map; understanding why a building nearby looks bigger than a building further away; understanding how the rails of a railway track appear to meet at the horizon – all these questions are relevant for students within this overarching idea.

As students live in a three-dimensional space, they should be familiar with views of objects from three orthogonal aspects (for example the front, the side, and from above). They should be aware of the power and limitations of different representations of three-dimensional shapes as indicated by the example provided in the following Figure 1.7. Not only must they understand the relative position of objects, but also how they can navigate through space and through constructions and shapes. An example would be reading and interpreting a map and designing instructions on how to get from point A to point B using coordinates, common language or a picture.

Conceptual understanding of shapes also includes the ability to take a three-dimensional object and make a two-dimensional net of it, and vice-versa, even if the three-dimensional object is presented in two dimensions. An example of this is given in the following Figure 1.8.

In conclusion, here is a list of key aspects of *space and shape*:

- recognising shapes and patterns;

- describing, encoding and decoding visual information;

- understanding dynamic changes to shapes;

- similarities and differences;

- relative positions;

- 2-D and 3-D representations and the relations between them;

- navigation through space.

Examples

Figure 1.6 shows a simple example of the need for flexibility in seeing shapes as they change. It is based on a cube that is being "sectioned" (that is, plane cuts are made through the cube). A variety of questions could be asked, such as:

What shapes can be produced by one plane cut through a cube?

How many faces, edges, or vertices will be produced when a cube is sectioned in this way?

Figure 1.6 ■ **A cube, with plane cuts in various places**

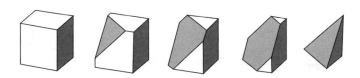

Three examples of the need for familiarity with representations of three-dimensional shapes follow. In the first example, the side and front view of an object constructed of cubes is given in Figure 1.7. The question is:

How many cubes have been used to make this object?

Figure 1.7 ■ **Side and front views of an object made from cubes**

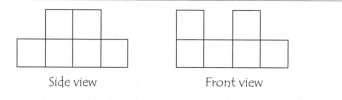

Side view   Front view

It may come as a surprise to many – students and teachers alike – that the maximum number of cubes is 20 and the minimum is 6, (de Lange, 1995).

The next example shows a two-dimensional representation of a barn, and an incomplete net of the barn. The problem is to complete the net of the barn.

Figure 1.8 ■ **Two-dimensional representation of a three-dimensional barn, and its (incomplete) net**

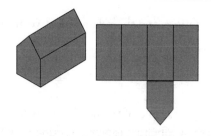

A final example similar to the previous one is shown in the following Figure 1.9. (adapted from Hershkovitz *et al.*, 1996).

Figure 1.9 ■ **Cube with black bottom**

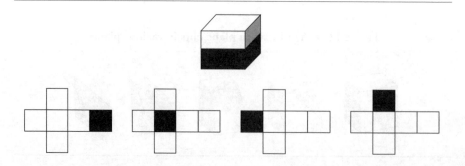

The lower half of the cube has been painted black. For each of the four nets, the bottom side is already black. Students could be asked to finish each net by shading the right squares.

Change and relationships

Description

In order to be sensitive to the patterns of change, Stewart (1990) states that we need to:

- represent changes in a comprehensible form;

- understand the fundamental types of change;

- recognise particular types of change when they occur;

- apply these techniques to the outside world;

- control a changing universe to our best advantage.

Change and relationships can be represented visually in a variety of ways: numerically (for example in a table), symbolically or graphically. Translation between these representations is of key importance, as is the recognition of an understanding of fundamental relationships and types of change. Students should be aware of the concepts of linear growth (additive process), exponential growth (multiplicative process) and periodic growth, as well as logistic growth, at least informally as a special case of exponential growth.

Students should also see the relationships among these models – the key differences between linear and exponential processes, the fact that percentage growth is identical with exponential growth, how logistic growth occurs and why, either in continuous or discrete situations.

Changes occur in a system of interrelated objects or phenomena where the elements influence each other. In the examples mentioned in the summary, all phenomena changed over time. But there are many examples in real life of matters in which objects are interrelated in a multitude of ways. For example:

If the length of the string of a guitar is halved, the new tone is an octave higher than the original tone. The tone is therefore dependent on the string length.

When we deposit money into a bank account, we know that the account balance will depend on the size, frequency and number of deposits and withdrawals, and the interest rates.

Relationships lead to dependency. Dependency concerns the fact that properties and changes of certain mathematical objects may depend on or influence properties and changes of other mathematical objects. Mathematical relationships often take the form of equations or inequalities, but relations of a more general nature may appear as well.

Change and relationships involves functional thinking. For 15-year-olds this includes students having a notion of rate of change, gradients and steepness (although not necessarily in a formal way), and dependence of one variable on another. They should be able to make judgements about how fast processes are taking place, also in a relative way.

This overarching idea closely relates to aspects of other overarching ideas. The study of patterns in numbers can lead to intriguing relationships: the study of Fibonacci numbers and the Golden Ratio are examples. The Golden Ratio is a concept that plays a role in geometry as well. Many more examples of *change and relationships* can be found in *space and shape*: the growth of an area in relation to the growth of a perimeter or diameter. Euclidean geometry lends itself also to the study of relationships. A well-known example is the relationship between the three sides of a triangle. If the length of two sides is known, the third is not determined, but the interval in which it lies is known: the interval's endpoints are the absolute value of the difference between the other two sides, and their sum, respectively. Several other similar relationships exist for the various elements of a triangle.

Uncertainty lends itself to various problems that can be viewed from the perspective of *change and relationships*. If two fair dice have been rolled and one of them shows four, what is the chance that the sum exceeds seven? The answer (50%) relies on the dependency of the probability at issue on the set of favourable outcomes. The required probability is the proportion of all such outcomes compared with all possible outcomes, which is a functional dependency.

Examples

School excursion

A school class wants to rent a coach for an excursion, and three companies are contacted for information about prices.

Company A charges an initial rate of 375 zed plus 0.5 zed per kilometre driven. Company B charges an initial rate of 250 zed plus 0.75 zed per kilometre driven. Company C charges a flat rate of 350 zed up to 200 kilometres, plus 1.02 zed per kilometre beyond 200 km.

Which company should the class choose, if the excursion involves a total travel distance of somewhere between 400 and 600 km?

Leaving aside the fictitious elements of the context, this problem could conceivably occur. Its solution requires the formulation and activation of several functional relationships, and equations and inequations. It can be dealt with by graphical as well as algebraic means, or combinations of both. The fact that the total travel distance in the excursion is not known exactly also introduces links to the *uncertainty* overarching idea.

A graphical representation of the problem is presented in the following Figure 1.10.

Figure 1.10 ■ **Excursion charges for three bus companies**

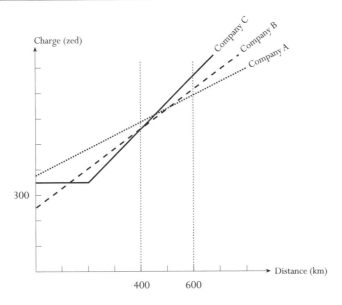

Cell growth

Doctors are monitoring the growth of cells. They are particularly interested in the day that the cell count will reach 60 000 because then they have to start an experiment. The table of results is:

Time (days)	4	6	8	10	12	14	16	18	20
Cells	597	893	1 339	1 995	2 976	2 976	14 719	21 956	32 763

When will the number of cells reach 60 000?

Prey-Predator

The following graph shows the growth of two living organisms – the Paramecium and Saccharomyces:

Paramecium

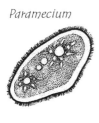

Saccharomyces

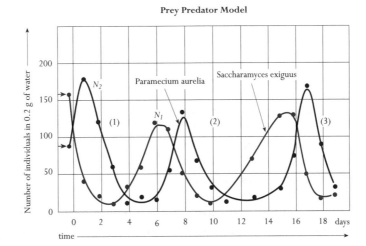

One of the two animals (predator) eats the other one (prey). Looking at the graph, can you judge which one is the prey and which one the predator?

One property of prey-predator phenomena is expressed as: The rate of growth of predators is proportional to the number of available prey. Does this property hold for the above graphs?

Uncertainty

Description

Science and technology rarely deal with certainty. The sciences are engaged in trying to find out how the world works, and to the degree that they succeed, so does our ability to describe with confidence what has happened in the past and to predict accurately what is likely to happen in the future. But scientific knowledge is rarely, if ever, absolute, not to mention sometimes being wrong, so there always remains some uncertainty in even the most scientific predictions.

The recommendations on the place of data, statistics and probability in school curricula emphasise data analysis. As a result, it is easy to view statistics in particular as a collection of specific skills. David S. Moore has pointed out what the overarching idea *uncertainty* really is all about. The OECD/PISA definition will follow his ideas as presented in *On the Shoulders of Giants* (Steen, 1990), and F. James Rutherford's as presented in *Why Numbers Count* (Steen, 1997).

The ability to deal intelligently with variation and uncertainty is the goal of instruction about data and chance. Variation is a concept that is hard to deal with: children who begin their education with spelling and multiplication expect the world to be deterministic; they learn quickly to expect one answer to be right and others wrong, at least when the answers take numerical form. Variation is unexpected and uncomfortable.

Statistics brings something to mathematics education that is unique and important: reasoning from uncertain empirical data. This kind of statistical thinking should be part of the mental equipment of every intelligent citizen. The core elements are:

- the omnipresence of variation in processes;

- the need for data about processes;

- the design of data production with variation in mind;

- the quantification of variation;

- the explanation of variation.

Data are not merely numbers, but numbers in a context. Data thus engage our knowledge of their context so that we can understand and interpret, rather than simply carry out arithmetical operations. Statistics in the early grades is taught not primarily for its own sake, but because it is an effective way to develop quantitative understanding and reasoning and to apply arithmetic and graphing to problem solving.

Collecting good data on important issues is no easy task. For the OECD/PISA study, the data must be interesting, relevant and practical, and carry a meaning for the students.

Data are obtained by measuring some characteristic, which means to represent it by a number. Thinking about measurement leads to a mature grasp of why some numbers are informative and others are irrelevant or nonsensical. First, what is a valid way to measure? Length is reasonably easy – a ruler will usually do it to a sufficient degree of accuracy for many purposes. But for area there may be a problem, since even for physical measurements uncertainty plays a role. Not only is the instrument important, but also the required degree of accuracy and the variability of measures.

The design of sample surveys is a core topic in statistics. Data analysis emphasises understanding the specific data at hand, assuming they represent a larger population. The concept of simple random samples is essential for 15-year-olds to understand the issues related to uncertainty.

A well known example:

In 1975, Ann Landers, a famous advice columnist, asked her readers:

"If you had to do it all over again, would you have children?"

10 000 people responded with 70% saying: NO.

It is well known that with voluntary responses, the overwhelming number come from people with strong (negative) feelings. A nationwide random sample about the same question rendered that 90% of the parents would like to have children again.

The essence of data analysis is to "let the data speak" by looking for patterns without first considering whether the data are representative of some larger universe.

Phenomena have uncertain individual outcomes and frequently the pattern of repeated outcomes is random. It has been shown that our intuition of chance profoundly contradicts the laws of probability (Garfield & Ahlgren, 1988; Tversky & Kahneman, 1974). This is in part due to the limited contact of students with randomness. The study of data offers a natural setting for such an experience. This explains why the priority of data analysis over formal probability and inference should be an important principle for the learning and teaching of uncertainty. Even at the college level, many students fail to understand probability and inference because of misconceptions that are not removed by study of formal rules. The concept of probability in the present OECD/PISA study will generally be based to situations regarding chance devices like coins, number cubes and spinners, or not too complex real-world situations that can be analysed intuitively, or can feasibly be modelled with these devices.

Uncertainty also appears from sources like natural variation in students' heights, reading scores, incomes of a group of people, etc. A step that is very important, even for 15-year-olds, is to see the study of data and chance as a coherent whole. One such principle is the progression of ideas from simple data analysis to data production to probability to inference.

The important specific mathematical concepts and activities in this area are:

- producing data – what are valid ways to measure particular characteristics and are the data valid for the proposed use? Critical attitude plays a very important role here, as does the design of the statistical study;

- data analysis and data display/visualisation, graphic representations of data, numerical descriptions like mean and median;

- probability;

- inference, which plays a minor role for students concerned in the study because formal treatment and specific methods are normally reserved for upper-grade secondary courses.

Examples

The following examples illustrate the *uncertainty* overarching idea.

Average age

If 40% of the population of a country are at least 60 years old, is it then possible for the average age to be 30?

Growing incomes?

Has the income of people in Zedland gone up or down in recent decades? The median money income per household fell: in 1970 it was 34 200 zed, in 1980 it was 30 500 zed and in 1990 31 200 zed. But the income per person increased: in 1970 13 500 zed, in 1980 13 850, and in 1990 15 777 zed.

A household consists of all people living together at the same address. Explain how it is possible for the household income to go down at he same time the per-person income has risen in Zedland.

Rising crimes

The following graph was taken from the weekly Zedland *News Magazine*:

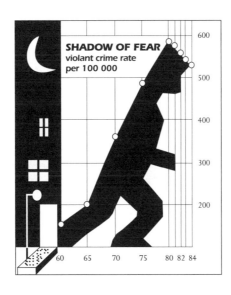

It shows the number of reported crimes per 100 000 inhabitants, starting with five-year intervals, then changing to one-year intervals.

How many reported crimes per 100 000 were there in 1960?

Manufacturers of alarm systems used the same data to produce the following graph:

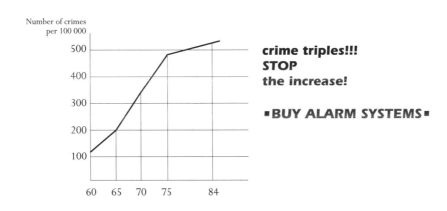

How did the designers come up with this graph and why?

The police were not too happy with the graph from the alarm systems manufacturers because the police want to show how successful crime fighting has been.

Design a graph to be used by the police to demonstrate that crime has decreased recently. ⌐

Reading Literacy

DEFINITION OF THE DOMAIN

Definitions of reading and reading literacy have changed over time in parallel with changes in society, the economy and culture. The concept of learning, and particularly the concept of lifelong learning, has expanded perceptions of reading literacy and the demands made on it. Literacy is no longer considered an ability only acquired in childhood during the early years of schooling. Instead, it is viewed as an expanding set of knowledge, skills and strategies which individuals build on throughout life in various situations, and through interaction with their peers and with the larger communities in which they participate.

Through a consensus-building process involving the reading experts selected by the participating countries and the OECD/PISA advisory groups, the following definition of reading literacy was adopted for the survey:

"Reading literacy is understanding, using and reflecting on written texts, in order to achieve one's goals, to develop one's knowledge and potential and to participate in society."

This definition goes beyond the notion of reading literacy as decoding and literal comprehension: it implies that reading literacy involves understanding, using and reflecting on written information for a variety of purposes. It thus takes into account the active and interactive role of the reader in gaining meaning from written texts. The definition also recognises the full scope of situations in which reading literacy plays a role for young adults, from private to public, from school to work, from active citizenship to lifelong learning. It spells out the idea that literacy enables the fulfilment of individual aspirations – from defined aspirations such as gaining an educational qualification or obtaining a job, to those less immediate goals which enrich and extend one's personal life. Literacy also provides the reader with a set of linguistic tools that are increasingly important for meeting the demands of modern societies with their formal institutions, large bureaucracies and complex legal systems.

Readers respond to a given text in a variety of ways as they seek to use and understand what they are reading. This dynamic process involves many factors, some of which can be manipulated in large-scale assessments such as OECD/PISA. These include the reading situation, the structure of the text itself and the characteristics of the questions that are asked about the text (the test rubric). All of these factors are regarded as important components of the reading process and were manipulated in the creation of the items used in the assessment.

In order to use text format, characteristics of the items and situations in constructing the assessment tasks, and later in interpreting the results, the range for each of these factors had to be specified. This allowed for the categorisation of each task so that the weighting of each component could be taken into account in the final assembly of the survey.

TEXT FORMAT

At the heart of the OECD/PISA assessment is a distinction between continuous and non-continuous texts.

- *Continuous texts* are typically composed of sentences that are, in turn, organised into paragraphs. These may fit into even larger structures such as sections, chapters and books. The primary classification of continuous texts is by rhetorical purpose, or text type.

- *Non-continuous texts* (or documents, as they are known in some approaches) can be categorised in two ways. One is the formal structure approach used in the work of Kirsch and Mosenthal (1989-1991). Their work classifies texts by the way underlying lists are put together to construct the various non-continuous text types. This approach is useful for understanding the similarities and differences between types of non-continuous texts. The other method of classification is by everyday descriptions of the formats of these texts. This second approach is used in classifying non-continuous texts in OECD/PISA.

Continuous texts

Text types are standard ways of organising continuous texts by content and author's purpose.

- *Narration* is the type of text in which the information refers to properties of objects in time. Narrative texts typically provide answers to "when", or "in what sequence" questions.

- *Exposition* is the type of text in which the information is presented as composite concepts or mental constructs, or elements into which concepts or mental constructs can be analysed. The text provides an explanation of how the component elements interrelate in a meaningful whole and often answers "how" questions.

- *Description* is the type of text in which the information refers to properties of objects in space. Descriptive texts typically provide an answer to "what" questions.

- *Argumentation* is the type of text that presents propositions as to the relationship between concepts, or other propositions. Argumentative texts often answer "why" questions. Another important sub-classification of argumentative texts is persuasive texts.

- *Instruction* (sometimes called injunction) is the type of text that provides directions on what to do and includes procedures, rules, regulations and statutes specifying certain behaviours.

- A *document or record* is a text that is designed to standardise and conserve information. It can be characterised by highly formalised textual and formatting features.

- *Hypertext* is a set of text slots linked together in such a way that the units can be read in different sequences, allowing readers to follow various routes to the information.

Non-continuous texts

Non-continuous texts are organised differently from continuous texts and so require different kinds of reading approaches. The reader should refer to the work of Kirsch and Mosenthal (1989-1991) for a discussion of the structural approach. According to their work, lists are the most elementary non-continuous texts. They consist of a number of entries that share some property(ies). This shared property may be used as a label or title for the list. Lists may have their entries ordered (*e.g.*, the names of students in a class arranged alphabetically) or unordered (*e.g.*, a list of supplies to be bought at a shop).

Classifying non-continuous texts by their format, as shown below, provides a familiar means of discussing what types of non-continuous texts may be included in the assessment.

- *Charts and graphs* are iconic representations of data. They are used for the purposes of scientific argumentation, and also in journals and newspapers to display numerical and tabular public information in a visual format.

- *Tables and matrices*. Tables are row and column matrices. Typically, all the entries in each column and each row share properties and thus the column and row labels are part of the information structure of the text. Common tables include schedules, spreadsheets, order forms and indexes.

- *Diagrams* often accompany technical descriptions (*e.g.*, demonstrating parts of a household appliance), expository texts and instructive texts (*e.g.*, illustrating how to assemble a household appliance). It is often useful to distinguish procedural (how to) from process (how something works) diagrams.

- *Maps* are non-continuous texts that indicate the geographical relationships between places. There is a variety of types of maps. Road maps mark the distance and routes between identified places. Thematic maps indicate the relationships between locations and social or physical features.

- *Forms* are structured and formatted texts which request the reader to respond to specific questions in specified ways. Forms are used by many organisations to collect data. They often contain structured or pre-coded answer formats. Typical examples are tax forms, immigration forms, visa forms, application forms, statistical questionnaires, etc.

- *Information sheets* differ from forms in that they provide, rather than request, information. They summarise information in a structured way and in such a format that the reader can easily and quickly locate specific pieces of information. Information sheets may contain various text forms as well as lists, tables, figures and sophisticated text-based graphics (headings, fonts, indentation, borders, etc.) to summarise and highlight information. Timetables, price lists, catalogues and programmes are examples of this type of non-continuous text.

- *Calls and advertisements* are documents designed to invite the reader to do something, *e.g.*, to buy goods or services, attend gatherings or meetings, elect a person to a public office, etc. The purpose of these documents is to persuade the reader. They offer something and request both attention and action. Advertisements, invitations, summonses, warnings and notices are examples of this document format.

- *Vouchers* testify that their owner is entitled to certain services. The information that they contain must be sufficient to show whether the voucher is valid or not. Typical examples are tickets, invoices, etc.

- *Certificates* are written acknowledgements of the validity of an agreement or a contract. They are formalised in content rather than format. They require the signature of one or more persons authorised and competent to bear testimony of the truth of the given statement. Warranties, school certificates, diplomas, contracts, etc. are documents that have these properties.

Figure 2.1 ■ **Distribution of reading literacy tasks, by text format and type**

Reading as a major domain (PISA 2000)

Reading as a minor domain (PISA 2003)

Text format and type	Percentage of tasks by text format and type (%)		Percentage of tasks by text format and type, based on the whole test (%)	
■ *Continuous*				
Narrative	21	17	14	11
Expository	36	67	24	43
Descriptive	14	17	9	11
Argumentative and persuasive	20	-	13	-
Injunctive	10	-	7	-
TOTAL[1]	**100**	**100**	**68**	**64**
■ *Non-Continuous*				
Charts and graphs	37	20	12	7
Tables	29	40	9	14
Diagrams	12	-	4	-
Maps	10	10	3	4
Forms	10	30	3	11
Advertisements	2	-	1	-
TOTAL[1]	**100**	**100**	**32**	**36**

1. Data may not always add up to the totals indicated because of roundings.

The distribution and variety of texts that students are asked to read for OECD/PISA are important characteristics of the assessment. Figure 2.1 shows the distributions of tasks for continuous and non-continuous texts in PISA 2000 (reading as major domain) and in PISA 2003 (reading as minor domain). It can be readily seen that in both 2000 and 2003 continuous texts represent two-thirds of the tasks or items contained in the assessment. Within this category, in both cycles, the largest percentage comes from expository texts.

CHARACTERISTICS OF THE ITEMS

Three sets of variables are used to describe the characteristics of the items: the processes (aspects), which set out the task for the examinee; item types, which set out the ways in which examinees are asked to demonstrate their proficiency at the task; and rules for marking, which specify how examinees' answers are to be evaluated. Each of these will be discussed in turn, though the first requires considerably more attention.

Five processes (aspects)

In an effort to simulate authentic reading situations, the OECD/PISA reading assessment measures the following five processes associated with achieving a full understanding of a text, whether the text is continuous or non-continuous. Examinees are expected to demonstrate their proficiency in all of these processes:

- retrieving information,
- forming a broad general understanding,
- developing an interpretation,
- reflecting on and evaluating the content of a text, and
- reflecting on and evaluating the form of a text.

The full understanding of texts involves all of these processes. It is expected that all readers, irrespective of their overall proficiency, will be able to demonstrate some level of competency in each of them (Langer, 1995). While there is an interrelationship between the five aspects – each may require many of the same underlying skills – successfully accomplishing one may not ensure successful completion of any other. Some view them as being in the repertoire of each reader at every developmental level rather than forming a sequential hierarchy or set of skills.

Figure 2.2 identifies the key distinguishing characteristics of the five processes of reading measured in OECD/PISA. While this figure necessarily oversimplifies each process, it provides a useful scheme for organising and remembering the relationships between them. As depicted in this figure, the five processes can be distinguished in terms of four characteristics. The first deals with the extent to which the reader is expected to use information primarily from within the text or to draw also upon outside knowledge.

Figure 2.2 ■ **Characteristics distinguishing the five processes (aspects) of reading literacy**

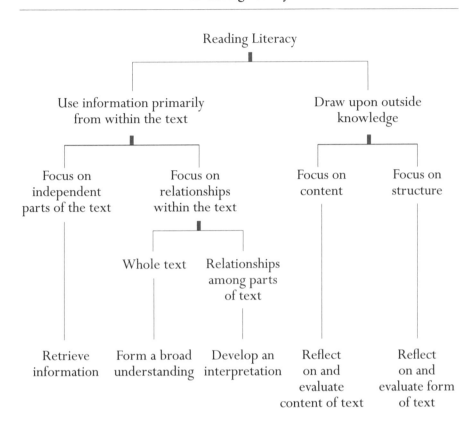

A second characteristic involves the extent to which the reader is asked to focus on independent parts of the text or on the relationships within the information contained in the text. Sometimes readers are expected to retrieve independent pieces of information while at other times they are asked to demonstrate their understanding of the relationships between parts of the text. Focusing on either the whole text or on relationships between parts of the text is the third distinguishing characteristic. The fourth characteristic relates to whether the reader is asked to deal with the content or substance of the text rather than its form or structure. The five processes of reading are represented in the last line of Figure 2.2 at the ends of the various branches. By starting at the top of the figure and following each branch one can see which characteristics are associated with each process.

The following discussion attempts to define each process operationally and to associate it with particular kinds of items. Although each process is discussed in terms of a single text, each can also apply to multiple texts when these are presented together as a unit within the test. The description of each process has two parts. The first provides a general overview of the process, while the second describes particular ways in which the process might be assessed.

Retrieving information

In the course of daily life, readers often need a particular piece of information: a telephone number or the departure time for a bus or train. They may want to find a particular fact to support or refute a claim someone has made. In situations such as these, readers are interested in retrieving isolated pieces of information. To do so, readers must scan, search for, locate and select relevant information. The processing involved is most frequently at the sentence level, though in some cases the information may be in two or more sentences or in different paragraphs.

In assessment tasks that call for retrieving information, examinees must match information given in the question with either identically worded or synonymous information in the text and use this to find the new information called for. In these tasks, retrieving information is based on the text itself and on explicit information included in it. Retrieving tasks require the examinee to find information based on requirements or features specified in questions. The examinee has to detect or identify one or more essential elements of a question: characters, place/time, setting, etc. and then to search for a match that may be literal or synonymous.

Retrieving tasks can involve various degrees of ambiguity. For example, the examinee may be required to select explicit information, such as an indication of time or place in a text or table. A more difficult version of this same type of task might involve finding synonymous information. This sometimes involves categorisation skills, or it may require discriminating between two similar pieces of information. The different levels of proficiency associated with this process of comprehension can be measured by systematically varying the elements that contribute to the difficulty of the task.

Forming a broad general understanding

To form a broad general understanding of what has been read, a reader must consider the text as a whole or in a broad perspective. There are various assessment tasks in which readers are asked to form a broad general understanding. Examinees may demonstrate initial understanding by identifying the main topic or message or by identifying the general purpose or use of the text. Examples include tasks that require the reader to select or create a title or thesis for the text, to explain the order of simple instructions, or to identify the main dimensions of a graph or a table. Others include tasks that require the examinee to describe the main character, setting or milieu of a story, to identify a theme or message of a literary text, or to explain the purpose or use of a map or a figure.

Within this process some tasks might require the examinee to match a particular piece of text to the question. For example, this would happen when a theme or main idea is explicitly stated in the text. Other tasks may require the examinee to focus on more than one specific reference in the text – for instance, if the reader had to deduce the theme from the repetition of a particular category of information. Selecting the main idea implies establishing a hierarchy among ideas and choosing the most general and overarching. Such a task indicates whether the examinee can distinguish between key ideas and minor details, or can recognise the summary of the main theme in a sentence or title.

Developing an interpretation

Developing an interpretation requires readers to extend their initial impressions so that they develop a more specific or complete understanding of what they have read. Tasks in this category call for logical understanding; readers must process the organisation of information in the text. To do so, readers must demonstrate their understanding of cohesion even if they cannot explicitly state what cohesion is. In some instances, developing an interpretation may require the reader to process a sequence of just two sentences relying on local cohesion, which might even be facilitated by the presence of cohesive markers, such as the use of "first" and "second" to indicate a sequence. In more difficult instances (*e.g.*, to indicate relations of cause and effect), there might not be any explicit markings.

Examples of tasks that might be used to assess this process include comparing and contrasting information, drawing inferences, and identifying and listing supporting evidence. "Compare and contrast" tasks require the examinee to draw together two or more pieces of information from the text. In order to process either explicit or implicit information from one or more sources in such tasks, the reader must often infer an intended relationship or category. This process of comprehension is also assessed in tasks that require the examinee to make inferences about the author's intention, and to identify the evidence used to infer that intention.

Reflecting on and evaluating the content of a text

Reflecting on and evaluating the content of a text requires the reader to connect information in a text to knowledge from other sources. Readers must also assess the claims made in the text against their own knowledge of the world. Often readers are asked to articulate and defend their own points of view. To do so, readers must be able to develop an understanding of what is said and intended in a text. They must then test that mental representation against what they know and believe on the basis of either prior information, or information found in other texts. Readers must call on supporting evidence from within the text and contrast that with other sources of information, using both general and specific knowledge as well as the ability to reason abstractly.

Assessment tasks representative of this category of processing include providing evidence or arguments from outside the text, assessing the relevance of particular pieces of information or evidence, or drawing comparisons with moral or aesthetic rules (standards). The examinee might be asked to offer or identify alternative pieces of information that might strengthen an author's argument, or to evaluate the sufficiency of the evidence or information provided in the text.

The outside knowledge to which textual information is to be connected may come from the examinee's own knowledge, from other texts provided in the assessment, or from ideas explicitly provided in the question.

Reflecting on and evaluating the form of a text

Tasks in this category require readers to stand apart from the text, consider it objectively and evaluate its quality and appropriateness. Knowledge of such things as text structure, genre and register play an important role in these tasks. These features, which form the basis of an author's craft, figure strongly in understanding standards inherent in tasks of this nature. Evaluating how successful an author is in portraying some characteristic or persuading a reader depends not only on substantive knowledge but also on the ability to detect nuances in language – for example, understanding when the choice of an adjective might colour interpretation.

Some examples of assessment tasks characteristic of reflecting on the form of a text include determining the utility of a particular text for a specified purpose and evaluating an author's use of particular textual features in accomplishing a particular goal. The examinee may also be called upon to describe or comment on the author's use of style and to identify the author's purpose and attitude.

Figure 2.3 shows the distribution of reading literacy tasks by each of the three subscales generated from the five reading processes (aspects) defined above. The largest category of tasks, which accounts for approximately 50 per cent of the test, is represented by the two branches of Figure 2.2 that ask students to focus on relationships within a text. These tasks require students either to form a broad understanding or to develop an interpretation. They have been grouped together for reporting purposes into a single process called interpreting texts. In PISA 2000 and 2003, the next largest category was made up of the 29 per cent of the tasks that require students to demonstrate their skill at retrieving isolated pieces of information. Each of these processes – forming a broad understanding, retrieving information and developing an interpretation – focuses on the degree to which the reader can understand and use information contained primarily

Figure 2.3 ■ **Distribution of reading literacy tasks, by reading process (aspect)**

Reading as a major domain (PISA 2000)

Reading as a minor domain (PISA 2003 and 2006)

Reading process (aspect)	Percentage of tasks (%)	
Retrieving information	29	29
Interpreting texts	49	50
Reflection and evaluation	22	21
TOTAL	**100**	**100**

within the text. The remaining of the tasks approximately 20 per cent required students to reflect on either the content or information provided in the text or on the structure and form of the text itself.

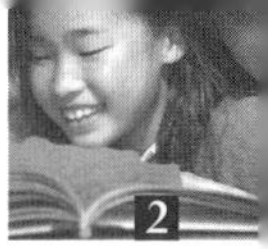

Item types

Figure 2.4 indicates that in PISA 2000 and 2003, around 43 per cent of the reading literacy tasks in the OECD/PISA assessment were open constructed-response items which required judgement on the part of the marker. The remaining tasks consist of closed constructed-response items that require little judgement on the part of the marker, as well as simple multiple-choice items, for which students choose one of several alternative answers, and complex multiple-choice items, for which students choose more than one response.

This table also reveals that while multiple-choice and open constructed-response items are represented across the processes, they are not distributed evenly. A larger percentage of multiple-choice items are associated with the two processes dealing with interpreting relationships within a text. This is shown in the second row of Figure 2.4. In contrast, while reflection and evaluation tasks account for around 20 per cent in PISA 2000 and 2003, only 2 per cent in 2000 are multiple-choice. Of the reflection and evaluation tasks, around 20 per cent are open constructed-response items that require judgement on the part of the marker.

Figure 2.4 ■ **Distribution of reading literacy tasks, by reading process (aspect) and item type**

Reading as a major domain (PISA 2000)

Reading as a minor domain (PISA 2003)

	Item types									
Process (aspect)	Percentage of multiple-choice items		Percentage of complex multiple-choice items		Percentage of closed constructed-response items		Percentage of open constructed-response items[1]		TOTAL[2]	
Retrieving information	8		2	4	6	14	13	11	29	29
Interpreting texts	32	29	2	4	2	7	13	11	49	50
Reflection and evaluation	2		2				18	21	22	21
TOTAL[2]	42	29	6	7	9	21	44	43	100	100

1. This category includes short-response items.

2. Data may not always add up to the totals indicated because of rounding.

Marking

Marking is relatively simple with dichotomously scored multiple-choice items: the examinee has either chosen the designated answer or not. Partial-credit models allow for more complex marking of items. Here, because some wrong answers are more complete than others, examinees who provide an "almost right" answer receive partial credit. Psychometric models for such polytomous scoring are well-established and in some ways are preferable to dichotomous scoring, as they utilise more of the information in the responses. Interpretation of polytomous marking is more complex, however, as each task has several locations on the difficulty scale: one for the full-credit answer and others for each of the partial-credit answers. Partial-credit marking is used for some of the more complex constructed-response items in OECD/PISA.

SITUATIONS

The manner in which situation was defined was borrowed from the Council of Europe's (2001) work on language. Four situation variables were identified: reading for private use, reading for public use, reading for work and reading for education. While the intention of the OECD/PISA reading literacy assessment was to measure the kinds of reading that occur both within and outside classrooms, the manner in which situation was defined could not be based simply on where the reading activity is carried out. For example, textbooks are read both in schools and in homes, and the process and purpose of reading these texts differ little from one setting to another. Moreover, reading also involves the author's intended use, different types of content and the fact that others (*e.g.,* teachers and employers) sometimes decide what should be read and for what purpose.

Thus, for the purpose of this assessment, situation can be understood as a general categorisation of texts based on the author's intended use, on the relationship with other persons implicitly or explicitly associated with the text, and on the general content. The sample texts were drawn from a variety of situations to maximise the diversity of content included in the reading literacy survey. Close attention was also paid to the origin of texts selected for inclusion in this survey. The goal was to reach a balance between the broad definition of reading literacy used in OECD/PISA and the linguistic and cultural diversity of participating countries. This diversity helped to ensure that no one group would be either advantaged or disadvantaged by the assessment content.

The four situation variables taken from the work of the Council of Europe can be described as follows:

- *Reading for private use (personal).* This type of reading is carried out to satisfy an individual's own interests, both practical and intellectual. It also includes reading to maintain or develop personal connections to other people. Contents typically include personal letters, fiction, biography and informational texts read for curiosity, as a part of leisure or recreational activities.

- *Reading for public use.* This type of reading is carried out to participate in the activities of the wider society. It includes the use of official documents as well as information about public events. In general, these tasks are associated with more or less anonymous contact with others.

- *Reading for work (occupational).* While not all 15-year-olds will actually have to read at work, it is important to assess their readiness to move into the world of work since, in most countries, over 50% of them will be in the labour force within one to two years. The prototypical tasks of this type are often referred to as "reading to do" (Sticht, 1975; Stiggins, 1982) in that they are tied to the accomplishment of some immediate task.

- *Reading for education.* This type of reading is normally involved with acquiring information as part of a larger learning task. The materials are often not chosen by the reader, but assigned by a teacher. The content is usually designed specifically for the purpose of instruction. The prototypical tasks are those usually identified as "reading to learn" (Sticht, 1975; Stiggins, 1982).

Figure 2.5 shows the distribution of reading literacy tasks in the assessment across all four situations for two scenarios: when reading was a major domain (PISA 2000) and when it is a minor domain (PISA 2003). A more even distribution of tasks across situations is achieved in 2003.

Figure 2.5 ■ **Distribution of reading literacy tasks, by situation**

Reading as a major domain (PISA 2000)

Reading as a minor domain (PISA 2003)

Situation	Percentage of tasks	
Personal	20	21
Public	38	25
Occupational	14	25
Educational	28	29
TOTAL	100	100

REPORTING OUTCOMES

Scaling the reading literacy tasks

The reading literacy tasks are constructed and administered to nationally representative samples of 15-year-olds in participating countries to ensure that the assessment provides the broadest possible coverage of reading literacy as defined here. However, no individual student can be expected to respond to the entire set of tasks. Accordingly, the survey is designed to give each student participating in the study a subset of the total pool of tasks, while at the same time ensuring that each of the tasks is administered to nationally representative samples of students. Summarising the performance of students across this entire pool of tasks thus poses a challenge.

One may imagine the reading literacy tasks arranged along a continuum in terms of difficulty for students and the level of skill required to answer each item correctly. The procedure used in OECD/PISA to capture this continuum of difficulty and ability is Item Response Theory (IRT). IRT is a mathematical model used for estimating the probability that a particular person will respond correctly to a given task from a specified pool of tasks. This probability is modelled along a continuum which summarises both the proficiency of a person in terms of his or her ability and the complexity of an item in terms of its difficulty. This continuum of difficulty and proficiency is referred to as a "scale".

Reporting

PISA 2003 will follow the reporting scheme used in PISA 2000, which reported outcomes in terms of a proficiency scale based on theory and interpretable in policy terms. The results of the reading literacy assessment were first summarised on a single composite reading literacy scale having a mean of 500 and a standard deviation of 100. In addition, student performance was also represented on five subscales: three process (aspect) subscales (retrieving information, interpreting texts, and reflection and evaluation; OECD, 2001a) and two text format subscales (continuous and non-continuous text; OECD, 2002b). These five subscales make it possible to compare mean scores and distributions among subgroups and countries by various components of the reading literacy construct. Although there is a high correlation between these subscales, reporting results on each subscale may reveal interesting interactions among the participating countries. Where such features occur, they can be examined and linked to the curriculum and teaching methodology used. In some countries, the important question may be how to teach the current curriculum better. In others, the question may not only be *how* to teach but also *what* to teach.

The reading process (aspect) subscales

Figure 2.6 summarises the reading literacy tasks in terms of three processes. There are two reasons for reducing the number of process subscales from five to three for reporting purposes. The first is pragmatic. In 2003 and 2006 reading, as a minor domain, will be restricted to about 30 items instead of the 141 that were used in 2000 when reading was a major domain. The amount of information, therefore, will be insufficient to report trends over five process subscales. The second reason is conceptual. The three process subscales are based on the set of five processes shown in Figure 2.2. *Forming a broad understanding* and *developing an interpretation* have been grouped together in an "interpreting texts" subscale because, in both, the reader processes information in the text: in the case of *forming a broad understanding*, the whole text and in the case of *developing an interpretation*, one part of the text in relation to another. *Reflecting on and evaluating the content of a text* and *reflecting on and evaluating the form of a text* have been collapsed into a single "reflection and evaluation" subscale because the distinction between reflecting on and evaluating content and reflecting on and evaluating form, in practice, was found to be somewhat arbitrary.

Figure 2.6 ■ **Relationship between the reading literacy framework and the process (aspect) subscales**

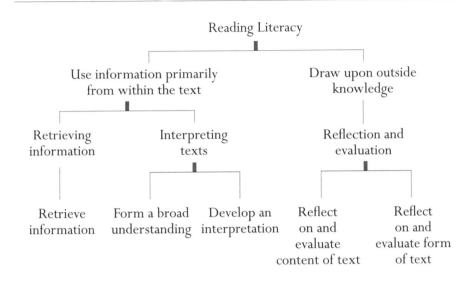

The text format subscales

PISA 2003 will also offer the possibility of providing results based on text format subscales, as reported in *Reading for change: Performance and engagement across countries* (OECD, 2002b). Figure 2.7 summarises the various text formats and the associated tasks along the two text format subscales. Organising the data in this way provides the opportunity to examine to what extent countries differ with respect to ability to deal with texts in different formats. In reporting results for 2000, two-thirds of the tasks were used to create the continuous text subscale while the remaining one-third of the tasks were used to create the non-continuous text subscale. There is a similar distribution of tasks between the two text formats in 2003.

Figure 2.7 ■ **Relationship between the reading literacy framework and the text format subscales**

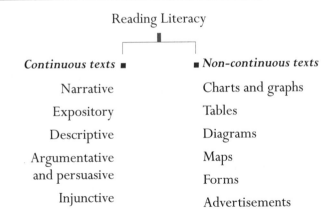

The scores on the composite scale as well as on each of the five subscales represent varying degrees of proficiency. A low score indicates that a student has very limited knowledge and skills, while a high score indicates that a student has quite advanced knowledge and skills. Use of Item Response Theory makes it possible not only to summarise results for various subpopulations of students, but also to determine the relative difficulty of the reading literacy tasks included in the survey. In other words, just as individuals receive a specific value on a scale according to their performance in the assessment tasks, each task receives a specific value on a scale according to its difficulty, as determined by the performance of students across the various countries that participate in the assessment.

Building an item map

The complete set of reading literacy tasks used in OECD/PISA varies widely in text format, situation and task requirements, and hence also in difficulty. This range is captured through what is known as an item map. The item map provides a visual representation of the reading literacy skills demonstrated by students along the scales. The map should contain a brief description of a selected number of released assessment tasks along with their scale values. These descriptions take into consideration the specific skills the item is designed to assess and, in the case of open-ended tasks, the criteria used for judging the item correct. An examination of the descriptions provides some insight into the range of processes required of students and the proficiencies they need to demonstrate at various points along the reading literacy scales.

Figure 2.8 shows an example of an item map from PISA 2000. An explanation of how to interpret it may be useful. The score assigned to each item is based on the theory that someone at a given point on the scale is equally proficient in all tasks at that point on the scale. It was decided that, for the purposes of OECD/PISA, "proficiency" should mean that students at a particular point on the reading literacy scale would have a 62 per cent chance of responding correctly to items at that point. For example, in Figure 2.8 an item appears at 421 on the composite scale. This means that students scoring 421 on the composite reading literacy scale will have a 62 per cent chance of correctly answering items graded 421 on the scale. This does not mean that students receiving scores below 421 will always answer incorrectly. Rather, students scoring below 421 will be expected to answer correctly an item of that level of difficulty less than 62 per cent of the time. Conversely, students having scores above 421 will have a greater than 62 per cent chance of responding correctly. It should be noted that the item will also appear on a process subscale and on a format subscale as well as on the combined reading literacy scale. In this example, the item at 421 on the composite scale requires students to identify the purpose that two short texts have in common by comparing the main ideas in each of them. It is an interpretation item and thus appears on the interpreting texts scale as well as on the continuous texts scale.

Figure 2.8 ■ **An example of a PISA 2000 item map**

Composite item map	Types of Process (Aspect)			Text Format	
	Retrieving Information	Interpreting	Reflecting and evaluating	Continuous	Non-continuous

○ Types of Process (Aspect)

■ Text Format

Composite item map	Retrieving Information	Interpreting	Reflecting and evaluating	Continuous	Non-continuous
822: **HYPOTHESISE** about an unexpected phenomenon by taking account of outside knowledge along with all relevant information in a **COMPLEX TABLE** on a relatively unfamiliar topic. (score 2)			○		■
727: **ANALYSE** several described cases and **MATCH** to categories given in a **TREE DIAGRAM**, where some of the relevant information is in footnotes. (score 2)		○			■
705: **HYPOTHESISE** about an unexpected phenomenon by taking account of outside knowledge along with some relevant information in a **COMPLEX TABLE** on a relatively unfamiliar topic. (score 1)			○		■
652: **EVALUATE** the ending of a **LONG NARRATIVE** in relation to its implicit theme or mood (score 2)			○	■	
645: **RELATE NUANCES OF LANGUAGE** in a **LONG NARRATIVE** to the main theme, in the presence of conflicting ideas. (score 2)		○		■	
631: **LOCATE** information in a **TREE DIAGRAM** using information in a footnote. (score 2)	○				■
603: **CONSTRUE** the meaning of a sentence by relating it to broad context in a **LONG NARRATIVE**.		○		■	
600: **HYPOTHESISE** about an authorial decision by relating evidence in a graph to the inferred main theme of **MULTIPLE GRAPHIC DISPLAYS**.			○		■
581: **COMPARE AND EVALUATE** the style of two open **LETTERS**.			○	■	
567: **EVALUATE** the ending of a **LONG NARRATIVE** in relation to the plot. (score 1)			○	■	
542: **INFER AN ANALOGICAL RELATIONSHIP** between two phenomena discussed in an open **LETTER**.		○		■	
540: **IDENTIFY** the implied starting date of a **GRAPH**.	○				■
539: **CONSTRUE THE MEANING** of short quotations from a **LONG NARRATIVE** in relation to atmosphere or immediate situation. (score 1)		○		■	
537: **CONNECT** evidence from a **LONG NARRATIVE** to personal concepts in order to justify opposing points of view. (score 2)			○	■	...

Figure 2.8 *(continued)* ■ **An example of a PISA 2000 item map**

○ Types of Process (Aspect)

■ Text Format

Composite item map	Retrieving Information	Interpreting	Reflecting and evaluating	Continuous	Non-continuous
529: EXPLAIN a character's motivation by linking events in a **LONG NARRATIVE**.		○		■	
508: INFER THE RELATIONSHIP between **TWO GRAPHIC DISPLAYS** with different conventions.		○			■
486: EVALUATE the suitability of a **TREE DIAGRAM** for particular purposes.			○		■
485: LOCATE numerical information in a **TREE DIAGRAM**. (score 1)	○				■
480: CONNECT evidence from a **LONG NARRATIVE** to personal concepts in order to justify a single point of view. (score 1)			○	■	
478: LOCATE AND COMBINE information in a **LINE GRAPH** and its introduction to infer a missing value.	○				■
477: UNDERSTAND the structure of a **TREE DIAGRAM**.		○			■
473: MATCH categories given in a **TREE DIAGRAM** to described cases, when some of the relevant information is in footnotes. (score 1)		○			■
447: INTERPRET information in a single paragraph to understand the setting of a **NARRATIVE**.		○		■	
445: Distinguish between variables and **STRUCTURAL FEATURES** of a **TREE DIAGRAM**.			○		■
421: IDENTIFY the common **PURPOSE** of **TWO SHORT TEXTS**.		○		■	
405: LOCATE pieces of explicit information in a **TEXT** containing strong organizers.	○			■	
397: Infer the **MAIN IDEA** of a simple **BAR GRAPH** from its title.		○			■
392: LOCATE a literal piece of information in a **TEXT** with clear text structure.	○			■	
367: LOCATE explicit information in a short, specified section of a **NARRATIVE**.	○			■	
363: LOCATE an explicitly stated piece of information in a **TEXT** with headings.	○			■	
356: RECOGNISE THEME of an article having a clear subheading and considerable redundancy.		○		■	

The PISA 2003 Assessment Framework – Mathematics, Reading, Science and Problem Solving Knowledge and Skills © OECD 2003

Levels of reading literacy proficiency

Just as students within each country are sampled to represent the national population of 15-year-old students, each reading literacy task represents a class of tasks from the reading literacy domain. Hence, it represents: proficiency in a type of processing and in dealing with a type of text that 15-year-old students should have acquired. One obvious question is, what distinguishes tasks at the lower end of the scale from those in the middle and upper ranges of the scale? Also, do tasks that fall around the same place on the scale share some characteristics that result in their having similar levels of difficulty? Even a cursory review of the item map reveals that tasks at the lower end of each scale differ from those at the higher end. A more careful analysis of the range of tasks along each scale provides indications of an ordered set of information-processing skills and strategies. Members of the reading expert group examined each task to identify a set of variables that seemed to influence its difficulty. They found that difficulty is in part determined by the length, structure and complexity of the text itself. However, they also noted that in most reading units (a unit being a text and a set of questions), the questions range across the reading literacy scale. This means that while the structure of a text contributes to the difficulty of an item, what the reader has to do with that text, as defined by the question or directive, interacts with the text and affects the overall difficulty.

The members of the reading expert group and test developers identified a number of variables that can influence the difficulty of any reading literacy task. One salient factor is the process involved in retrieving information, developing an interpretation or reflecting on what has been read. Processes range in complexity and sophistication from making simple connections between pieces of information, to categorising ideas according to given criteria, and to critically evaluating and hypothesising about a section of text. In addition to the process called for, the difficulty of retrieving information tasks varies with the number of pieces of information to be included in the response, the number of criteria which the information must satisfy, and whether or not what is retrieved needs to be sequenced in a particular way. In the case of interpretative and reflective tasks, the amount of a text that needs to be assimilated is an important factor affecting difficulty. In items that require reflection on the reader's part, difficulty is also conditioned by the familiarity or specificity of the knowledge that must be drawn on from outside the text. In all processes of reading, the difficulty of the task depends on how prominent the required information is, how much competing information is present, and whether or not the reader is explicitly directed to the ideas or information required to complete the task.

In an attempt to capture this progression of complexity and difficulty in PISA 2000, the composite reading literacy scale and each of the subscales were divided into five levels:

Level	Score points on the PISA scale
1	335 to 407
2	408 to 480
3	481 to 552
4	553 to 625
5	More than 625

Expert panels judged that the tasks within each level of reading literacy shared many of the same task features and requirements, and differed in systematic ways from tasks at higher or lower levels. As a result, these levels appear to be a useful way to explore the progression of reading literacy demands within each scale. This progression is summarised in Figure 2.9. This process will be repeated for the major domains for each cycle.

Figure 2.9 ■ **Reading literacy levels map**

Retrieving information	**Interpreting texts**	**Reflecting and evaluating**
5		
Locate and possibly sequence or combine multiple pieces of deeply embedded information, some of which may be outside the main body of the text. Infer which information in the text is relevant to the task. Deal with highly plausible and/or extensive competing information.	Either construe the meaning of nuanced language or demonstrate a full and detailed understanding of a text.	Critically evaluate or hypothesise, drawing on specialised knowledge. Deal with concepts that are contrary to expectations and draw on a deep understanding of long or complex texts.

Continuous texts: Negotiate texts whose discourse structure is not obvious or clearly marked, in order to discern the relationship of specific parts of the text to its implicit theme or intention.

Non-continuous texts: Identify patterns among many pieces of information presented in a display which may be long and detailed, sometimes by referring to information external to the display. The reader may need to realise independently that a full understanding of the section of text requires reference to a separate part of the same document, such as a footnote.

4		
Locate and possibly sequence or combine multiple pieces of embedded information, each of which may need to meet multiple criteria, in a text with familiar context or form. Infer which information in the text is relevant to the task.	Use a high level of text-based inference to understand and apply categories in an unfamiliar context, and to construe the meaning of a section of text by taking into account the text as a whole. Deal with ambiguities, ideas that are contrary to expectation and ideas that are negatively worded.	Use formal or public knowledge to hypothesise about or critically evaluate a text. Show accurate understanding of long or complex texts.

Continuous texts: Follow linguistic or thematic links over several paragraphs, often in the absence of clear discourse markers, in order to locate, interpret or evaluate embedded information or to infer psychological or metaphysical meaning.

Non-continuous texts: Scan a long, detailed text in order to find relevant information, often with little or no assistance from organisers such as labels or special formatting, to locate several pieces of information to be compared or combined.

Figure 2.9 *(continued)* ■ **Reading literacy levels map**

Retrieving information	Interpreting texts	Reflecting and evaluating
3		
Locate, and in some cases recognise the relationship between pieces of information, each of which may need to meet multiple criteria. Deal with prominent competing information.	Integrate several parts of a text in order to identify a main idea, understand a relationship or construe the meaning of a word or phrase. Compare, contrast or categorise taking many criteria into account. Deal with competing information.	Make connections or comparisons, give explanations, or evaluate a feature of text. Demonstrate a detailed understanding of the text in relation to familiar, everyday knowledge, or draw on less common knowledge.

Continuous texts: Use conventions of text organisation, where present, and follow implicit or explicit logical links such as cause and effect relationships across sentences or paragraphs in order to locate, interpret or evaluate information.

Non-continuous texts: Consider one display in the light of a second, separate document or display, possibly in a different format, or combine several pieces of spatial, verbal and numeric information in a graph or map to draw conclusions about the information represented.

Retrieving information	Interpreting texts	Reflecting and evaluating
2		
Locate one or more pieces of information, each of which may be required to meet multiple criteria. Deal with competing information.	Identify the main idea in a text, understand relationships, form or apply simple categories, or construe meaning within a limited part of the text when the information is not prominent and low-level inferences are required.	Make a comparison or connections between the text and outside knowledge, or explain a feature of the text by drawing on personal experience and attitudes.

Continuous texts: Follow logical and linguistic connections within a paragraph in order to locate or interpret information; or synthesise information across texts or parts of a text in order to infer the author's purpose.

Non-continuous texts: Demonstrate a grasp of the underlying structure of a visual display such as a simple tree diagram or table, or combine two pieces of information from a graph or table.

Retrieving information	Interpreting texts	Reflecting and evaluating
1		
Locate one or more independent pieces of explicitly stated information, typically meeting a single criterion, with little or no competing information in the text.	Recognise the main theme or author's purpose in a text about a familiar topic, when the required information in the text is not prominent.	Make a simple connection between information in the text and common, everyday knowledge.

Continuous texts: Use redundancy, paragraph headings or common print conventions to form an impression of the main idea of the text, or to locate information stated explicitly within a short section of text.

Non-continuous texts: Focus on discrete pieces of information, usually within a single display such as a simple map, a line graph or a bar graph that presents only a small amount of information in a straightforward way, and in which most of the verbal text is limited to a small number of words or phrases.

Interpreting the reading literacy levels

Not only does each level represent a range of tasks and associated knowledge and skills, it also represents a range of proficiencies demonstrated by students. As mentioned previously, the reading literacy levels were initially set by the members of the reading expert group to represent a set of tasks with shared characteristics. These levels also have shared statistical properties. The average student within each level can be expected to successfully perform the average task within that level 62 per cent of the time. In addition, the width of each level is in part determined by the expectation that a student at the lower end of any level will score 50 per cent on any hypothetical test made up of items randomly selected from that level.

Since each reading literacy scale represents a progression of knowledge and skills, students at a particular level not only demonstrate the knowledge and skills associated with that particular level but the proficiencies associated with the lower levels as well. Thus the knowledge and skills assumed at each level build on and encompass the proficiencies laid down in the next lower level. This means that a student who is judged to be at Level 3 on a reading literacy scale is proficient not only in Level 3 tasks but also in Level 1 and 2 tasks. This also means that students who are at Levels 1 and 2 will be expected to get the average Level 3 item correct less than 50 per cent of the time. Put another way, they will be expected to score less than 50 per cent on a test made up of items drawn from Level 3.

Figure 2.10 shows the probability that individuals performing at selected points along the combined reading literacy scale will give a correct response to tasks of varying difficulty. One is a Level 1 task, one is a Level 3 task, and the third task receives two score points: one at Level 4 and the other at Level 5. It is readily seen here that a student with a score of 298, who is estimated to be below Level 1, has only a 43 per cent chance of responding correctly to the Level 1 task that is at 367 on the reading literacy scale. This person has only a 14 per cent chance of responding to the item from Level 3 and almost no chance of responding correctly to the item from Level 5. Someone with a proficiency of 371, in the middle of Level 1, has a 63 per cent chance of responding to the item at 367, but only slightly more than one chance in four of responding correctly to the task at 508, and only a seven per cent chance of responding correctly to the task selected from Level 5. In contrast, someone at Level 3 would be expected to respond correctly 89 per cent of the time to tasks at 367 on the reading literacy scale, and 64 per cent of the time to tasks at 508, near the middle of Level 3. However, he or she would only have just over one chance in four (27 per cent) of correctly responding to items from the middle of Level 5. Finally, a student at Level 5 is expected to respond correctly most of the time to most of the tasks. As shown in Figure 2.10, a student having a score of 662 on the combined reading literacy scale has a 98 per cent chance of answering the task at 367 correctly, a 90 per cent chance of answering the item at Level 3 (508) correctly and a 65 per cent of responding correctly to the task selected from near the centre of Level 5 (652).

Figure 2.10 ■ **Probability (as a percentage) of responding correctly to selected tasks of varying difficulty for students with varying levels of proficiency**

	Level 1 item at 367 points	Level 3 item at 508 points	Level 4 item at 567 points	Level 5 item at 652 points
Below Level 1 *(Proficiency of 298 points)*	43	14	8	3
Level 1 *(Proficiency of 371 points)*	63	27	16	7
Level 2 *(Proficiency of 444 points)*	79	45	30	14
Level 3 *(Proficiency of 517 points)*	89	64	48	27
Level 4 *(Proficiency of 589 points)*	95	80	68	45
Level 5 *(Proficiency of 662 points)*	98	90	82	65

Figure 2.10 also implicitly raises questions concerning the highest and lowest designated levels. Even though the top of the reading literacy scale is unbounded, it can be stated with some certainty that students of extremely high proficiency are capable of performing tasks characterised by the highest level of proficiency. There is more of an issue for students who are at the bottom end of the reading literacy scale. Level 1 begins at 335, yet a certain percentage of students in each country is estimated to be below this point on the scale. While there are no reading literacy tasks with a scale value below 335, it is not correct to say that these students are without any reading literacy skills or are "totally illiterate". However, on the basis of their performance in the set of tasks used in this assessment, they would be expected to score less than 50 per cent on a set of tasks selected from Level 1. They are classified, therefore, as performing below Level 1.

Since comparatively few young adults in our societies have no literacy skills, the framework does not call for a measure of whether or not 15-year-old students can read in a technical sense. That is, OECD/PISA does not measure the extent to which 15-year-old students are fluent readers or how competent they are at word recognition tasks or spelling. It does, however, reflect the contemporary view that students should, upon completing compulsory education, be able to construct, extend and reflect on the meaning of what they have read across a wide range of continuous and non-continuous texts commonly associated with a variety of situations both within and outside school. While it was not possible to say what knowledge and skills students performing below Level 1 may possess with regard to reading literacy, their level of proficiency indicates that these students are unlikely to be able to use reading independently as a tool to assist them in acquiring knowledge and skills in other areas. ⌋

Scientific Literacy

An important life skill for young people is the capacity to draw appropriate and guarded conclusions from evidence and information given to them, to criticise claims made by others on the basis of the evidence put forward, and to distinguish opinion from evidence-based statements. Science has a particular part to play here since it is concerned with rationality in testing ideas and theories against evidence from the world around. This is not to say that science excludes creativity and imagination, which have always played a central part in advancing human understanding of the world. Ideas which sometimes appear to have "come out of the blue" have been seized upon by a mechanism which Einstein described as "the way of intuition, which is helped by a feeling for the order lying behind the appearance" (Einstein, 1933). Which ideas are "seized upon" has depended historically upon their social acceptability at that time, so that developments in scientific knowledge depend not only on the creativity of individuals but also on the culture in which they are proposed. But once the creative leap is made and a new theoretical framework for understanding has been articulated, then it has to be followed by painstaking testing against reality. As Hawking (1988) has written:

"A theory is a good theory if it satisfies two requirements: it must accurately describe a large class of observations on the basis of a model that contains only a few arbitrary elements, and it must make definite predictions about the results of future observations" (Hawking ,1988, p. 9).

Theories that do not meet these requirements, or cannot be tested, are not scientific theories. It is important for an educated citizen to be able to distinguish between the kinds of questions that can be answered by science and those which cannot, and between what is scientific and what is pseudo-scientific.

DEFINITION OF THE DOMAIN

Current thinking about the desired outcomes of science education for all citizens emphasises the development of a general understanding of important concepts and explanatory frameworks of science, of the methods by which science derives evidence to support claims for its knowledge, and of the strengths and limitations of science in the real world. It values the ability to apply this understanding to real situations involving science in which claims need to be assessed and decisions made. For example, Millar and Osborne (1998) have identified the focus of a modern science curriculum as being: "the ability to read and assimilate scientific and technical information and assess its significance". Their report continues:

"In this approach, the emphasis is not on how to 'do science'. It is not on how to create scientific knowledge, or to recall it briefly for a terminal examination. ...Thus, in science, students should be asked to demonstrate a capacity to evaluate evidence, to distinguish theories from observations and to assess the level of certainty ascribed to the claims advanced" (Millar & Osborne, 1998).

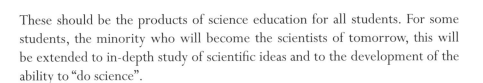

These should be the products of science education for all students. For some students, the minority who will become the scientists of tomorrow, this will be extended to in-depth study of scientific ideas and to the development of the ability to "do science".

With these points in mind, it is considered that the essential goal of science education, which should be the focus of OECD/PISA, is that students should be scientifically literate. This term has been used in different contexts. For example, the International Forum on Scientific and Technological Literacy for All (UNESCO, 1993) offered a variety of views, such as:

> *"The capability to function with understanding and confidence, and at appropriate levels, in ways that bring about empowerment in the made world and in the world of scientific and technological ideas"* (UNESCO, 1993).

Included in the many different views of scientific literacy (reviewed by Shamos, 1995; Laugksch, 2000; see also Graeber & Bolte, 1997) are notions of levels of scientific literacy. For example, Bybee (1997) has proposed four levels, of which the lowest two are "nominal scientific literacy", consisting of knowledge of names and terms, and "functional literacy", which applies to those who can use scientific vocabulary in limited contexts. These are seen as being at levels too low to be aims within the OECD/PISA framework. The highest level identified by Bybee, "multidimensional scientific literacy", includes understanding of the nature of science and of its history and role in culture, at a level most appropriate for a scientific elite rather than for all citizens. It is, perhaps, the assumption that scientific literacy involves thinking at this level of specialisation that causes difficulty in communicating a more attainable notion of it. What is more appropriate for the purposes of the OECD/PISA science framework is closer to Bybee's third level, "conceptual and procedural scientific literacy".

Having considered a number of existing descriptions, OECD/PISA defines scientific literacy as follows:

> *Scientific literacy is the capacity to use scientific knowledge, to identify questions and to draw evidence-based conclusions in order to understand and help make decisions about the natural world and the changes made to it through human activity.*

The following remarks further explain the meaning condensed in this statement.

Scientific literacy…

It is important to emphasise not only that both scientific knowledge (in the sense of knowledge about science) and the processes by which this knowledge is developed are essential for scientific literacy, but that they are bound together in this understanding of the term. As discussed in more detail below, the processes are only scientific when they are used in relation to the subject matter of science. Thus, using scientific processes necessarily involves some understanding of the scientific subject matter. The view of scientific literacy adopted here acknowledges this combination of ways of thinking about, and understanding, the scientific aspects of the world.

…use scientific knowledge to identify questions and to draw evidence-based conclusions…

In the above definition, scientific knowledge is used to mean far more than knowledge of facts, names and terms. It includes understanding of fundamental scientific concepts, the limitations of scientific knowledge and the nature of science as a human activity. The questions to be identified are those that can be answered by scientific enquiry, implying knowledge about science as well as about the scientific aspects of specific topics. Drawing evidence-based conclusions means knowing and applying processes of selecting and evaluating information and data, whilst recognising that there is often not sufficient information to draw definite conclusions, thus making it necessary to speculate, cautiously and consciously, about the information that is available.

…understand and help make decisions…

This phrase indicates first, that an understanding of the natural world is valued as a goal in itself as well as being necessary for decision-making and, second, that scientific understanding can contribute to, but rarely determines, decision making. Practical decisions are always set in situations having social, political or economic dimensions, and scientific knowledge is used in the context of human values related to these dimensions. Where there is agreement about the values in a situation, the use of scientific evidence can be non-controversial. Where values differ, the selection and use of scientific evidence in decision making will be more controversial.

…the natural world and the changes made to it through human activity…

The phrase *the natural world* is used as shorthand for the physical setting, living things and the relationships among them. Decisions about the natural world include those associated with science related to self and family, community and global issues. Changes made through human activity refer to planned and unplanned adaptations of the natural world for human purposes (simple and complex technologies) and their consequences.

It is relevant to note here, and will be made more explicit later, that scientific literacy is not a dichotomy. That is, it is not suggested that people can be categorised as being either scientifically literate or scientifically illiterate. Rather, there is a progression from less developed to more developed scientific literacy. For example, the student with less developed scientific literacy might be able to recall simple scientific factual knowledge (*e.g.,* names, facts, terminology, simple rules) and to use common science knowledge in drawing or evaluating conclusions. A more developed scientific literacy will show in being able to create or use simple conceptual models to make predictions or give explanations, to make and communicate them with precision, to analyse scientific investigations in relation to experimental design, to use data as evidence to evaluate alternative viewpoints or different perspectives and their implications, and to communicate evaluations with precision.

ORGANISATION OF THE DOMAIN

The OECD/PISA definition of scientific literacy comprises three aspects:

- *Scientific knowledge or concepts,* which will be assessed by application to specific subject matter;

- *Scientific processes* which, because they are scientific, will involve knowledge of science, although in the assessment this knowledge must not form the major barrier to success;

- *Situations or context* in which the knowledge and processes are assessed and which take the form of science-based issues.

Although these aspects of scientific literacy are discussed separately, it must be recognised that, in the assessment of scientific literacy, there will always be a combination of all three.

The first two of these aspects are used both for the construction of test items and for the characterisation of student performance. The third aspect ensures that in the development of the assessment items, due attention is paid to situating the science in a diverse range of relevant settings.

The following sections elaborate the three organising aspects. In laying out these aspects, the OECD/PISA framework has ensured that the focus of the assessment is upon the outcome of science education as a whole.

Scientific knowledge or concepts

Only a sample of scientific ideas can be assessed. Moreover, the purpose of OECD/PISA is not to report on all the knowledge that students may have, but to describe the extent to which they can apply their knowledge in contexts of relevance to their present and future lives. No attempt is made to identify a full list of knowledge that might be included, but rather to specify the criteria for selection. Thus the knowledge that is assessed is selected from the major fields of physics, chemistry, biological science and Earth and space science according to the following three criteria.

- The first of these is relevance to everyday situations. Scientific knowledge differs in the degree to which it is useful in every-day life. For example, although the theory of relativity gives a more accurate description of the relationships between length, mass, time and velocity, Newton's laws are more helpful in matters relating to the understanding of forces and motion encountered every day.

- The second criterion is that the knowledge and areas of application selected should have enduring relevance to life throughout the next decade and beyond. Given that the major assessment of science is planned to take place in the year 2006, this cycle of OECD/PISA will focus on the knowledge likely to remain important in science and public policy for a number of years.

- The third criterion is that the knowledge required can be combined with selected scientific processes. This would not be the case where only recall of a label or of a definition was involved.

Figure 3.1 shows the outcome of applying these criteria to the content of the major fields of science. It lists major scientific themes, with a few examples of the knowledge relating to them. This knowledge is required for understanding the natural world and for making sense of new experience. It depends upon and derives from study of specific phenomena and events but goes beyond the detailed knowledge that comes from study of these things. The examples listed in Figure 3.1 are given to convey the meanings of the themes; there is no attempt to list comprehensively all the knowledge that could be related to each theme.

Figure 3.1 ■ **Major scientific themes for the assessment of scientific literacy**

- Structure and properties of matter (thermal and electrical conductivity)
- Atmospheric change (radiation, transmission, pressure)
- Chemical and physical changes (state of matter, rates of reaction, decomposition)
- Energy transformations (energy conservation, energy degradation, photosynthesis)
- Forces and movement (balanced/unbalanced forces, velocity, acceleration, momentum)
- Form and function (cell, skeleton, adaptation)
- Human biology (health, hygiene, nutrition)
- Physiological change (hormones, electrolysis, neurons)
- Biodiversity (species, gene pool, evolution)
- Genetic control (dominance, inheritance)
- Ecosystems (food chains, sustainability)
- The Earth and its place in the universe (solar system, diurnal and seasonal changes)
- Geographical change (continental drift, weathering)

Scientific processes

Processes are mental (and sometimes physical) actions used in conceiving, obtaining, interpreting and using evidence or data to gain knowledge or understanding. Processes have to be used in relation to some subject matter; there is no meaning to a content-free process. They can be used in relation to a wide range of subject matter; they become scientific processes when the subject matter is drawn from scientific aspects of the world and the outcome of using them is to further scientific understanding.

What are commonly described as the processes of science range widely over the skills and understanding needed to collect and interpret evidence from the world around us and to draw conclusions from it. The processes related to collecting evidence include those concerned with investigation in practice – planning and setting up experimental situations, taking measurements and making observations using appropriate instruments, etc. The development of these processes is included in the aims of school science education so that students can experience and understand how scientific understanding is built up and, ideally, the nature of scientific enquiry and scientific knowledge. Few will require these practical skills in life after school, but they will need the understanding of processes and concepts developed through practical, hands-on enquiry. Moreover, it has been strongly argued that what is traditionally regarded as the "scientific process", by which conclusions are drawn inductively from observations, and which is still reflected in much school science, is contrary to how scientific knowledge is developed (*e.g.*, Ziman, 1980).

Scientific literacy, as identified here, gives higher priority to using scientific knowledge to "draw evidence-based conclusions" than to the ability to collect evidence for oneself. The ability to relate evidence or data to claims and conclusions is seen as central to what all citizens need in order to make judgements about the aspects of their lives that are influenced by science. It follows that every citizen needs to know when scientific knowledge is relevant, distinguishing between questions which science can and cannot answer. Every citizen needs to be able to judge when evidence is valid, both in terms of its relevance and how it has been collected. Most important of all, however, every citizen needs to be able to relate evidence to conclusions based on it and to be able to weigh the evidence for and against particular courses of action that affect life at a personal, social or global level.

The distinctions that have just been made can be summarised briefly as giving priority to processes *about* science as compared with processes *within* science. It is important that the process skills listed in Figure 3.2 be read as being primarily about science and not primarily as they apply within science. All of the processes listed in Figure 3.2 involve scientific knowledge. In the first process the scientific knowledge is the essential factor. In the second and third processes this knowledge is necessary but not sufficient, since knowledge about collecting and using scientific evidence and data is essential.

Figure 3.2 ■ **The PISA 2003 scientific processes**

Scientific Literacy

• Process 1: Describing, explaining and predicting scientific phenomena

• Process 2: Understanding scientific investigation

• Process 3: Interpreting scientific evidence and conclusions

Some elaboration of these processes follows.

Describing, explaining and predicting scientific phenomena

In this process students demonstrate their understanding by applying appropriate scientific knowledge in a given situation. It includes describing or explaining phenomena and predicting changes, and may involve recognising or identifying appropriate descriptions, explanations and predictions.

Understanding scientific investigation

Understanding scientific investigation involves recognising and communicating questions that can be investigated scientifically and knowing what is involved in such investigations. It includes recognising scientifically investigable questions or suggesting a question that could be investigated scientifically in a given situation. It also includes identifying or recognising evidence needed in a scientific investigation: for example, what things should be compared, what variables should be changed or controlled, what additional information is needed, or what action should be taken so that relevant data can be collected.

Interpreting scientific evidence and conclusions

This means making sense of scientific findings as evidence for claims or conclusions. It may involve accessing scientific information and producing and communicating conclusions based on scientific evidence. It may also involve selecting from and communicating about alternative conclusions in relation to the evidence; giving reasons for or against a given conclusion in terms of the data provided, or identifying the assumptions made in reaching a conclusion; and reflecting on and communicating the societal implications of scientific conclusions.

Some scientific knowledge is needed for all three processes. In the case of the second and third, however, the knowledge is not intended to be the main "hurdle", since the aim is to assess the mental processes involved in gathering, evaluating and communicating valid scientific evidence. In the first process, on the other hand, it is the understanding of the scientific ideas involved that is being assessed and this understanding is the main hurdle.

It is important to point out that, for each of the processes listed above, there is a wide range of item difficulty, depending upon the scientific knowledge and areas of application involved. The OECD/PISA assessments ensure that, through country feedback and the field trial, the items selected for the main study are at the appropriate level of difficulty for 15-year-olds.

Situations or context: the areas of application

As indicated earlier, OECD/PISA includes important scientific knowledge relevant to the science curricula of participating countries without being constrained by the common denominator of national curricula. In accordance

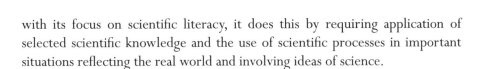

with its focus on scientific literacy, it does this by requiring application of selected scientific knowledge and the use of scientific processes in important situations reflecting the real world and involving ideas of science.

Figure 3.3 lists those areas of application of science that raise issues that the citizens of today and tomorrow need to understand and to make decisions about. It is these applications that guide the selection of content for units and the items within them. Figure 3.3 indicates the areas of application in which the scientific knowledge and processes will be assessed.

Figure 3.3 ■ **Areas of application for the science assessment**

- Science in life and health
  - Health, disease and nutrition
  - Maintenance of and sustainable use of species
  - Interdependence of physical/biological systems

- Science in Earth and environment
  - Pollution
  - Production and loss of soil
  - Weather and climate

- Science in technology
  - Biotechnology
  - Use of materials and waste disposal
  - Use of energy
  - Transportation

In framing test questions, it is necessary to consider not only the area of application, but also the setting in which the issue to be considered will be presented. In selecting the settings, it is important to keep in mind that the purpose of the assessment is to assess the ability of students to apply the skills and knowledge they have acquired by the end of the compulsory years of schooling. OECD/PISA requires that the assessment items should be framed in situations of life in general and not limited to life in school. In the school setting, scientific processes and knowledge may be confined to the laboratory or classroom, but increasingly an attempt is being made also in countries' science curricula to apply these to the world outside the school.

Real-world situations involve problems that can affect us as individuals (*e.g.*, food and energy use) or as members of a local community (*e.g.*, treatment of the water supply or siting of a power station) or as world citizens (*e.g.*, global warming, diminution of biodiversity). All of these are represented in the range of assessment items used in OECD/PISA. A further type of setting, appropriate to some topics, is the historical one, in which understanding of the advances in scientific knowledge can be assessed. In the framework of OECD/PISA the focus of the items is on matters relating to the self and family (personal), to the community (public), to life across the world (global), and on those that illustrate how scientific knowledge evolves and affects social decisions associated with science (historical relevance).

In an international study it is important that the areas of application used for assessment items should be chosen in the light of relevance to students' interests and lives in all countries. They should also be appropriate for assessing scientific processes and knowledge. Sensitivity to cultural differences has a high priority in item development and selection, not only for the sake of the validity of the assessment, but to respect the different values and traditions in participating countries. The areas of application chosen for the survey items are relevant and appropriate across the different countries, whilst involving the combination of scientific knowledge with the use of scientific processes.

By choosing these areas of application and settings, OECD/PISA is seeking to assess the application of knowledge most likely to have been gained in the science curriculum (although some may be gained from other subjects and from non-school sources). However, although the knowledge required is curricular knowledge, in order to find out if this has gone beyond learning isolated facts and is serving the development of scientific literacy, OECD/ PISA is assessing the application of that knowledge in items reflecting real-life situations. Some of the examples of items presented below help to convey this point.

TEST CHARACTERISTICS AND EXAMPLES

In accordance with the OECD/PISA definition of scientific literacy, each assessment question (item) will require the use of one of the processes in Figure 3.2 and, as has also been noted, some scientific knowledge. As the examples below illustrate, what is identified as a defined test unit will take the form of several items linked to some initial stimulus material. Although each item in a unit has been identified as mainly assessing one of the scientific processes listed in Figure 3.2, some items may also assess other scientific processes, and draw on various aspects of scientific knowledge.

One reason for this structure is to make the units as realistic as possible and to reflect in them to some extent the complexity of real-life situations. Another reason relates to the efficient use of testing time, cutting down on the time required for a student to "get into" the subject matter of the unit by having fewer situations, about which several questions can be posed, rather than separate questions about a larger number of different situations. The necessity to make each scored point independent of others within the unit is recognised and taken into account. It is also recognised that it is all the more important to minimise bias that may be due to the choice of situation when fewer situations are used.

Examples of the items for assessing some of these processes will help to convey their operational meaning.

Science Unit 1
STOP THAT GERM!

Process 2 is assessed in two questions within this unit. The students are asked to read a short text about the history of immunisation:

> As early as the 11th century, Chinese doctors were manipulating the immune system. By blowing pulverised scabs from a smallpox victim into their patients' nostrils, they could often induce a mild case of the disease that prevented a more severe onslaught later on. In the 1700s, people rubbed their skins with dried scabs to protect themselves from the disease. These primitive practices were introduced into England and the American colonies. In 1771 and 1772, during a smallpox epidemic, a Boston doctor named Zabdiel Boylston tested an idea that he had. He scratched the skin on his six-year-old son and 285 other people and rubbed pus from smallpox scabs into the wounds. All but six of his patients survived.

Science Example 1.1

What idea might Zabdiel Boylston have been testing?

Scoring and comments on Science Example 1.1

Full Credit

Code 2: Answers with reference both to:

- the idea that infecting someone with smallpox will provide some immunity;

AND

- the idea that by breaking the skin, the smallpox was introduced into the blood stream.

Partial Credit

Code 1: Answers which refer to either of the above points.

No Credit

Code 0: Other responses.

Item type: Open constructed-response
Process: Understanding scientific investigation (Process 2)
Concept: Human biology
Situation: Science in life and health

Science Example 1.2

Give two other pieces of information that you would need to decide how successful Boylston's approach was.

Scoring and comments on Science Example 1.2

Full Credit

Code 2: Answers that provide the following TWO pieces of information:

- the rate of survival without Boylston's treatment;

AND

- whether his patients were exposed to smallpox apart from the treatment.

Partial Credit

Code 1: Answers that provide either of the above points.

No Credit

Code 0: Other answers.

Item type: Open constructed-response
Process: Understanding scientific investigation (Process 2)
Concept: Human biology
Situation: Science in life and health

Science Unit 2
PETER CAIRNEY

The following four items are part of a unit for which the stimulus material is a passage about Peter Cairney, who works for the Australian Road Research Board. The stimulus material is presented below.

…Another way that Peter gathers information to improve road safety is by the use of a TV camera on a 13 metre pole to film the traffic on a narrow road. The pictures tell the researchers such things as how fast the traffic is going, how far apart the cars travel, and what part of the road the traffic uses. Then after a time, lane lines are painted on the road. The researchers can then use the TV camera to see whether the traffic is now different. Does the traffic now go faster or slower? Are the cars close together or further apart than before? Do the motorists drive closer to the edge of the road or closer to the centre now that the lines are there? When Peter knows these things he can give advice about whether or not to paint lines on narrow roads.

Science Example 2.1

If Peter wants to be sure that he is giving good advice, he might collect some other information as well beyond filming the narrow road. Which of these things would help him to be more sure about his advice concerning the effect of painting lines on narrow roads?

A. Doing the same on other narrow roads   Yes / No

B. Doing the same on wide roads   Yes / No

C. Checking the number of accidents in a certain time
   period before and after painting the lines   Yes / No

D. Checking the number of cars using the road before and after   Yes / No
   painting the lines

Scoring and comments on Science Example 2.1

Full Credit

Code 2: Answers that specify Yes, No, Yes, No, in that order.

Partial Credit

Code 1: Answers that specify Yes, No, No, No, in that order.

No Credit

Code 0: Any other combination of answers.

Item type: Complex multiple-choice
Process: Understanding scientific investigation (Process 2)
Concept: Forces and movement
Situation: Science in technology

Science Example 2.2

Suppose that on one stretch of narrow road Peter finds that after the lane lines are painted the traffic changes as below.

Speed   Traffic moves more quickly

Position   Traffic keeps nearer edges of road

Distance apart   No change

On the basis of these results it was decided that lane lines should be painted on all narrow roads. Do you think this was the best decision? Give your reasons for agreeing or disagreeing.

Agree: _____

Disagree: _____

Reason: _____

Scoring and comments on Science Example 2.2

Full Credit

Code 1: Answers that agree or disagree with the decision for reasons that are consistent with the given information. For example:

- agree because there is less chance of collisions if the traffic is keeping near the edges of the road, even if it is moving faster;

- agree because if traffic is moving faster, there is less incentive to overtake;

- disagree because if the traffic is moving faster and keeping the same distance apart, this may mean that the drivers don't have enough room to stop in an emergency.

No Credit

Code 0: Answers that agree or disagree without specifying the reasons, or provide reasons unrelated to the problem.

Item type: Open-constructed response
Process: Interpreting scientific evidence and conclusions (Process 3)
Concept: Forces and movement
Situation: Science in technology

Science Example 2.3

Drivers are advised to leave more space between their vehicles and the ones in front when they are travelling more quickly than when they are travelling more slowly because faster cars take longer to stop.

Explain why a faster car can take more distance to stop than a slower one.

Reasons: _____

Scoring and comments on Science Example 2.3

Full Credit

Code 2: Answers that mention that:

- the greater momentum of a vehicle when it is moving more quickly means that it will move further whilst slowing down than a slower vehicle, given the same force;

AND

- it takes longer to reduce speed to zero from a greater speed, so the car will travel further in this time.

Partial Credit

Code 1: Answers that mention only one of the above points.

No Credit

Code 0: Other responses, or repetition of the statement, *e.g.* that it takes longer to stop because of its speed.

Item type: Open constructed-response
Process: Describing, explaining and predicting scientific phenomena (Process 1)
Concept: Forces and movement
Situation: Science in technology

Science Example 2.4

Watching his TV, Peter sees one car A travelling at 45 km/h being overtaken by another car B travelling at 60 km/h. How fast does car B appear to be travelling to someone in car A?

A.   0 km/h
B.   15 km/h
C.   45 km/h
D.   60 km/h
E.   105 km/h

Scoring and comments on Science Example 2.4

Full Credit

Code 1: Response B: 15 km/h

No Credit

Code 0: Other responses.

Item type: Multiple-choice
Process: Describing, explaining and predicting scientific phenomena (Process 1)
Concept: Forces and movement
Situation: Science in technology

Science Unit 3
CORN

The following three items are from a unit entitled Corn. The stimulus material is a newspaper report about a man, Auke Ferwerda, who burns corn on his stove as a fuel.

…Ferwerda points out that corn, in the form of cattle food, is in fact a type of fuel too. Cows eat corn to get energy out of it. But, Ferwerda explains, the sale of corn for fuel instead of for cattle food might be much more profitable for farmers.

Ferwerda knows the environment is receiving increasing attention and government legislation to protect the environment is becoming increasingly elaborate. What Ferwerda does not quite understand is the amount of attention being focused on carbon dioxide. Carbon dioxide is regarded as the cause of the greenhouse effect. The greenhouse effect is said to be the main cause of the increasing average temperature of the Earth's atmosphere. In Ferwerda's view, however, there is nothing wrong with carbon dioxide. On the contrary, he argues, plants and trees absorb it and convert it into oxygen for human beings.

He says: "This is an agricultural area and the farmers grow corn. It has a long growing season, absorbs a lot of carbon dioxide and emits a lot of oxygen. There are many scientists who say that carbon dioxide is not the main cause of the greenhouse effect".

Science Example 3.1

Ferwerda compares corn used as fuel to corn used as food.

The first column of the table below contains a list of things that happen when corn burns as a fuel.

Do these things also happen when corn acts as a fuel in an animal body?

Circle Yes or No for each.

When corn burns:	Does this also happen when corn acts as a fuel in an animal body?
Oxygen is consumed.	Yes / No
Carbon dioxide is produced.	Yes / No
Energy is produced.	Yes / No

Scoring and comments on Science Example 3.1

Full Credit

Code 1: Answers that specify Yes, Yes, Yes, in that order. (All parts have to be answered correctly, since any one error would indicate some failure in understanding the process of using food in an animal body).

No Credit

Code 0: Answers which specify any other combination of responses.

Item type: Complex multiple-choice
Process: Describing, explaining and predicting scientific phenomena (Process 1)
Concept: Chemical and physical changes
Situation: Science in life and health

Science Example 3.2

In the article a conversion of carbon dioxide is described: "...plants and trees absorb it and convert it into oxygen ...".

There are more substances involved in this conversion than carbon dioxide and oxygen only. The conversion can be represented in the following way:

carbon dioxide + water ⟶ oxygen + [   ]

Write in the box the name of the missing substance.

Scoring and comments on Science Example 3.2

Full Credit

Code 1: Answers that mention any one of the following: glucose; sugar; carbohydrate(s); saccharide(s); starch.

No Credit

Code 0: Other responses.

Item type: Open constructed-response
Process: Describing, explaining and predicting scientific phenomena (Process 1)
Concept: Energy transformations
Situation: Science in life and health

Science Example 3.3

At the end of the article Ferwerda refers to scientists who say that carbon dioxide is not the main cause of the greenhouse effect.

Karin finds the following table in which research results about the four most important gases causing the greenhouse effect are listed.

Relative greenhouse effect per molecule of gas

Carbon dioxide	Methane	Nitrous oxide	Chlorofluorocarbons
1	30	160	17 000

From this table Karin concludes that carbon dioxide is not the main cause of the greenhouse effect. However this conclusion is premature. The data in the table need to be combined with other data to be able to conclude whether or not carbon dioxide is the main cause of the greenhouse effect. .

Which other data does Karin need to collect?

A. Data about the origin of the four gases.

B. Data about the absorption of the four gases by plants.

C. Data about the size of each of the four types of molecules.

D. Data about the amounts of each of the four gases in the atmosphere.

Scoring and comments on Science Example 3.3

There is a close relationship between the scientific knowledge that the concentration of a substance affects the extent of its action, and the recognition that a valid conclusion cannot be drawn without this extra information.

Full Credit

Code 1: Response D: Data about the amounts of each of the four gases in the atmosphere.

No Credit

Code 0: Other responses.

Item type: *Multiple-choice*
Process: *Interpreting scientific evidence and conclusions (Process 3)*
Concept: *Structure and properties of matter*
Situation: *Science in Earth and environment*

To answer all of these items the student is required to use knowledge that would be gained from the science curriculum and apply it in a novel situation. Where assessment of scientific understanding is not the main purpose of the item, the knowledge required is not the main challenge (or hurdle) and success should depend on ability in the particular process required. Where assessment of scientific understanding is the main aim, as in Science Examples 2.3, 2.4, 3.1 and 3.2, the process is one of demonstrating this understanding.

ASSESSMENT STRUCTURE

The test units incorporate up to about eight items, each independently scored. In the great majority of units, if not all, there are both items eliciting knowledge and understanding of the science involved, as in Science Examples 2.3 and 2.4 and 3.1 and 3.2, and items requiring use of one or more of the processes of collecting and using evidence and data in a scientific investigation, as in Science Examples 1.1, 1.2, 2.1, 2.2 and 3.3. As indicated earlier, OECD/PISA does not include practical ("hands on") units, at least in the years 2000 and 2003, when science is a "minor" domain.

For the overall assessment, the desired balance between the processes is given in terms of percentages of scored points and shown in Figure 3.4. This may be revised for the assessment in 2006, when science will be the major domain of OECD/PISA.

Figure 3.4 ▪ **Recommended distribution of scored points across science processes**

Scientific processes	Percentage of OECD/PISA science units
1. Describing, explaining and predicting scientific phenomena	40 – 50
2. Understanding scientific investigation	20 – 25
3. Interpreting scientific, evidence and conclusions	20 – 25
TOTAL	100

It may well be that the topics of some test units mean that the balance is tipped more towards assessment of understanding (Process 1), with the opposite occurring within other test units. Where possible, items assessing Processes 2 and 3 and items assessing Process 1 will occur within each unit. This is done both to achieve the aim of covering important scientific understanding that students are likely to have developed from their school science curricula or outside school, and because the ability to use processes is highly dependent upon the situation in which they are used. The aims of OECD/PISA suggest that both scientific knowledge and the combination of scientific knowledge with the ability to draw evidence-based conclusions are valued learning outcomes. The recommended target of roughly equal numbers of score points assigned to these two outcomes should serve these aims.

As already noted, all items will be concerned with the use of scientific knowledge that is likely to be developed in students through their school science curricula. Where the OECD/PISA science items differ from some – but by no means all – school science assessments is in their requirement that the knowledge be applied in real-life situations. Similarly, the ability to draw evidence-based conclusions appears among the aims of many school science curricula. The OECD/PISA assessment requires the application of the processes in situations that go beyond the school laboratory or classroom. The extent to which this is novel to students will depend on how far applications in the real world are part of the curriculum they have experienced.

Figure 3.5 ▪ **Recommended distribution of scored points across areas of application**

Areas of application	Percentage of OECD/PISA science units
Science in life and health	30 – 40
Science in Earth and environment	30 – 40
Science in technology	30 – 40
TOTAL	100

In relation to the areas of application, Figure 3.5 shows that there will be as even a spread as possible across the three main groups.

A test unit is defined by a particular stimulus material, which may be a short written passage, or writing accompanying a table, chart, graph or diagram. The items are a set of independently scored questions requiring selection of a response in a multiple-choice format, a short open response or a long open response. The difference between short and long open response is that the latter require multiple marking whilst the former can be marked reliably by only one marker.

Up to the present, when science is a minor domain in the surveys, the number of units and items developed and field-tested is limited. However, based on this experience, we can summarise the test format for 2003:

- With one exception, units are extended, not single items; they include items assessing one or more of the scientific knowledge or context (Figure 3.1), scientific processes (Figure 3.2), and knowledge relating to one or more areas of application of science (Figure 3.3), and require answers on paper (writing or drawing).

- Units are presented in written form for 2003 as in 2000, although the use of stimuli in other forms will be investigated for the year 2006, when science is the major element.

- Some units involve reading and/or mathematics, but there are no items that require only identification of information from the stimulus material without some additional scientific processing, nor items that require only the recall of isolated factual information.

To cover the range of skills and understanding identified in this framework requires a range of item response formats. For example, multiple-choice items can be produced that validly assess those processes involving recognition or selection. However, for assessing the ability to evaluate and communicate, an open-response format is more likely to provide validity and authenticity. In many cases, however, the most appropriate format depends on the particular content of the item.

REPORTING SCALES

To meet the aims of OECD/PISA, the development of scales of student achievement is essential. The process of arriving at a scale has to be iterative, so that initial descriptions based on the results of the trials and the 2000 survey - and informed by past experience of assessing science achievement and findings from research into learning and cognitive development in science – are likely to be modified as more data are accumulated in further trials and surveys.

PISA 2000, when science was a minor domain and thus provided limited information, reported scientific literacy in terms of a proficiency scale with a mean of 500 and a standard deviation of 100. Although no proficiency levels were identified, it was possible to describe what students can do in three points in this scale:

- Towards the top end of the scientific literacy scale (around 690 points) students are generally able to create or use conceptual models to make predictions or give explanations; to analyse scientific investigations in order to grasp, for example, the design of an experiment or to identify an idea being tested; to compare data in order to evaluate alternative viewpoints or differing perspectives; and to communicate scientific arguments and/or descriptions in detail and with precision.

- At around 550 points, students are typically able to use scientific knowledge to make predictions or provide explanations; to recognise questions that can be answered by scientific investigation and/or identify details of what is involved in a scientific investigation; and to select relevant information from competing data or chains of reasoning in drawing or evaluating conclusions.

- Towards the lower end of the scale (around 400 points), students are able to recall simple factual scientific knowledge (*e.g.* names, facts, terminology, simple rules), and to use common scientific knowledge in drawing or evaluating conclusions.

In 2003, the reporting of science results is likely to follow a similar format. However, in the year 2006, when the testing time available will permit a wider coverage of scientific knowledge and areas of application, it may be possible, in addition to adding specific cut-points identifying proficiency levels, to report sub-scales for the processes in Figure 3.2. This will include, therefore, a sub-scale relating to scientific knowledge (Process 1) to be assessed by application in the situations presented.

In 2006 there may also be sufficient information available across the scientific processes listed in Figure 3.2 to consider reporting performance in the major fields of science. This will depend on statistical, conceptual and policy considerations. If it proves feasible to report sub-scales, countries will have the benefit of being able to compare the achieved outcomes of their science education in detail with what they consider desirable outcomes.

Reporting on the content of, and incorrect responses to, different items is an important accompaniment to item statistics. It is expected that these content categories will be generated from the field trial and related to the kinds of answers actually given by students. Reporting some types of answers to specific items will also be necessary in order to illustrate the scales and to give meaningful labels to them. This will involve releasing some items from those used in OECD/PISA.

Further levels of reporting are desirable and may become possible after the major science survey in 2006. One of these is performance in groups of items across units relating to the separate areas of application of science. This information will be useful in considering whether sufficient and effective attention is being given to issues of current concern.

OTHER ISSUES

When information for a scientific literacy assessment unit is presented in the form of an extended written passage, aspects of reading can be assessed. Similarly, when information is presented in the form of tables, charts, graphs, etc., the ability to read information can be assessed, and where some manipulation of number is required, certain aspects of mathematics can be assessed. Such units will form part of the combined packages of the survey. Other units will assess only scientific processes involving drawing evidence-based conclusions and demonstrating scientific understanding.

The surveys of science in the years 2000 and 2003, in which science is a "minor" element, form the basis for comparisons over time. The restriction on the number of assessment units in 2000 and 2003 (even within a survey design that allows different packages of items to be answered by different sub-samples of students) means that there are fewer units relating to each area of application of science than will be possible in 2006. Thus the minor surveys of scientific literacy involve the assessment of all the processes identified in Figure 3.2 and some of the scientific knowledge (concepts) and areas of application identified in Figures 3.1 and 3.3. In the major year for science, 2006, a far more comprehensive coverage of the scientific knowledge and areas of application will be possible. ⌋

Problem Solving

INTRODUCTION

Problem solving is a central educational objective within every country's school program. Educators and policy makers are especially concerned about students' competencies for solving problems in real-life settings. That means understanding the information given, identifying the critical features and their interrelationships, constructing or applying an external representation, solving the problem, and evaluating, justifying and communicating their solutions. The processes of problem solving, so conceived, are found across the curriculum, in mathematics, the sciences, language arts, the social sciences, as well as in many other content areas. Problem solving provides a basis for future learning, for effectively participating in society and for conducting personal activities.

While problem solving is an ever-present human activity, the development of a framework to outline its components and develop measures of student performance is not easy. Several writers have commented on the lack of an agreed-upon comprehensive definition of problem solving (*e.g.*, Frensch & Funke, 1995; O'Neil, 1999). Yet there is a large body of literature on learning and related topics (Bransford, Brown, & Cocking, 1999; PEG, 2001) that discusses problem solving, often without giving an explicit definition of the term in context.

The OECD/PISA assessment programme develops, administers and interprets surveys of student literacy on an international basis. The expressed purpose of this programme is to monitor and report on student literacy levels in a number of domains. However, the focus of the programme is not on reporting the level of curricular knowledge the students have acquired. Rather, the programme focuses its efforts on describing the capabilities that students have in real-world situations that call for applications of their reading, science and mathematics knowledge and skills. Besides collecting data reflecting student performance in these literacy areas, the OECD/PISA 2003 assessment also collects data related to students' cross-disciplinary problem solving capabilities.

BACKGROUND

To prepare the OECD/PISA problem solving framework, an examination was made of extant, research-based programmes assessing student capabilities in solving problems set in novel surroundings. Several studies were identified as providing interesting results or utilising innovative formats. Among these were the following:

- the "clinical reasoning test" based on case studies in patient management (Boshuizen *et al.*, 1997);

- the "overall-test" of complex, authentic decision making in business education (Seger, 1997);

- the "what if – test", which addresses intuitive knowledge used in exploring simulations of science phenomena (Swaak & de Jong, 1996).

A more general review of research identified a range of relevant initiatives. For example, within mathematics there is a long tradition of the study of problem-oriented thinking and learning (Hiebert *et al.*, 1996; Schoenfeld, 1992) and related assessment strategies (Charles, Lester & O'Daffer, 1987; Dossey, Mullis, & Jones, 1993). In psychology, studies detail the importance of student knowledge of inductive reasoning (Csapó, 1997) and analogical reasoning (Vosniadou & Ortony, 1989). Klieme (1989) provides an integrated discussion of assessing problem solving from an educational, cognitive-psychological and measurement perspective. Collis, Romberg and Jurdak (1986) developed a problem solving test that used "super items," each of which was composed of a sequence of questions addressing subsequent levels of cognitive complexity. Another set of efforts deals with differentiating task complexity levels. Most of these build on the seminal work by Bloom, Hasting and Madaus (1971). Other promising efforts include the TIMSS performance expectations (Robitaille & Garden, 1996) and the various PISA assessment frameworks (OECD, 1999 & 2000).

In recent years there has been an increased interest in assessing problem solving as a cross-disciplinary competency, yet reviews of problem solving assessment (Klieme 2000; Mayer 1992) reveal no frameworks for it. During the past five years there have been several attempts to implement some cross-disciplinary problem solving in large-scale assessments. Trier and Peschar, working for OECD-Network A (1995), addressed problem solving as one of four important cross-disciplinary competencies. They conducted a feasibility test for such an assessment. Their sample "item" was an essay-like planning task, in which the subjects had to plan a trip for a youth club. While they were able to gather student data, they encountered difficulties in scoring the responses.

Working independently, Frensch and Funke (1995) devised several experimental variants of planning tests, while Klieme, *et al.* (in press) developed a multiple-choice test of problem solving competence for a large-scale assessment programme for one of the German federal states. In this assessment, the planning task was decomposed into action steps (clarifying goals, gathering information, planning, making decisions, executing the plan and evaluating the result). Each task was addressed by a sequence of items that required subjects to judge the consistency of goals; to analyse maps, schedules or other documents; to reason about the order of activities; to diagnose possible errors in the execution of actions; or other problem solving actions. A similar project approach to measuring student problem solving competencies is being considered for inclusion in the International Survey of Adults (ISA), formerly known as International Adult Literacy and Life Skills Survey (ALLS) (Binkley, *et al.*, 1999).

In a German national option involving 650 15-year-old students in PISA 2000, a set of eight cross-disciplinary problem solving assessments was implemented and validated (Klieme, 2000). The intention was to use as much input from basic cognitive research on problem solving as possible for the development and validation of new instruments. Results demonstrated the feasibility of both paper-and-pencil and computer-based instruments for cross-disciplinary problem solving assessment. The findings included that:

- cross-disciplinary problem solving competencies can be distinguished from domain-related competencies (mathematical literacy, scientific literacy and reading literacy);

- several indicators of analytical problem solving competence, including the "tyre pump task" designed by Harry O'Neill (1999), the "project approach" and a test with analogical transfer-problems, loaded on a common factor.

The objective of the OECD/PISA problem solving framework was to extend the prototypes developed in the feasibility and research studies to a workable model for a large-scale assessment as part of PISA 2003.

DEFINITION OF THE DOMAIN

Richard Mayer (1992) noted in writing about assessments of problem solving that designers must:

- require the problem-solver to engage in higher order thinking (or cognitive) processes with the goal of reaching solutions for realistic, authentic tasks that require the integration of skills; and

- confront the test taker with non-routine problems that require the student to invent a novel solution strategy.

The assessment of problem solving should extend into non-routine situations drawing on prior knowledge, merging content areas and requiring the integration of concepts, representations and processes on the part of test-takers.

Most people involved in the study of problem solving in research or practice-based settings, using one conception or another of the field, agree that in describing student problem solving, the major focus is on describing the cognitive acts students make in addressing, solving and reporting solutions. As such, PISA 2003 takes the following as its definition of problem solving:

Problem solving is an individual's capacity to use cognitive processes to confront and resolve real, cross-disciplinary situations where the solution path is not immediately obvious and where the literacy domains or curricular areas that might be applicable are not within a single domain of mathematics, science or reading.

Several terms in this definition need further explanation:

... cognitive processes ...

This aspect of problem solving deals with the various components of the problem solving act and the cognitive processes underlying them, including application of understanding, characterising, representing, solving, reflecting and communicating. These processes will be described in more detail in the next section.

... cross–disciplinary ...

In relation to problem solving, the current OECD/PISA assessments address problem solving within each domain. The frameworks of reading, mathematical, and scientific literacy assess problem solving skills within each of these domains. The OECD/PISA assessment of problem solving extends the consideration of student competencies to a broader range of problem solving items falling across the boundaries of traditional curricular areas.

... real ...

The above definition of problem solving emphasises solving real-life problems. These problems call on individuals to merge knowledge and strategies to confront and resolve a problem readily identifiable as arising from real-life situations. Such problems call on people to move among different, but sometimes related, representations and to exhibit some degree of flexibility in the way they retrieve and apply their knowledge. These problems call for students to make and communicate decisions that appear to have immediate ramifications for those involved.

ORGANISATION OF THE DOMAIN

With the OECD/PISA definition of problem solving, the tasks must necessarily depend on context- or domain-specific knowledge and strategies. Therefore, the contexts, domains and situations in which problem solving is assessed have to be selected very carefully. The following components need to be considered:

- *Problem types.* A general definition of problem solving would cover a wide spectrum of problem types. For the purpose of the PISA 2003 assessment, three problem types have been chosen: *decision making*, *system analysis and design*, and *trouble shooting*. A detailed discussion of these is included in the next section. These three problem types cover most of the problem solving processes generally identified within the problem solving domain. OECD/ PISA problem solving assessment does not include types such as interpersonal problem solving or argumentative text analysis.

- *Problem context.* This component involves the positioning of the problems relative to the students' experience with problem solving. In particular, the settings selected should be some distance from the classroom setting and students' school curricula. Hence, the PISA 2003 problems should employ contexts that involve personal life, work and leisure, and community and society. These contexts cover a continuum running from personal space to civic awareness, including both curricular and extra-curricular contexts.

- *Disciplines involved.* To reflect the real-life problem solving focus, the PISA 2003 problem solving domain will cover a wide range of disciplines including mathematics, science, literature, social studies, technology and commerce. As such, problem solving complements the main OECD/PISA domains of mathematical, scientific and reading literacy. The knowledge and skills involved in a problem solving task will not be restricted to any one of these domains, thus avoiding possible duplication.

- *Problem solving processes*. To what degree is the student able to confront a particular problem and begin to move toward a solution? What evidence does the student offer of understanding the nature of a problem, of characterising the problem through identification of variables and relationships, of selecting and adjusting representations of a problem, of moving to a solution, of reflecting on the work or of communicating the results?

- *Reasoning skills*. Each of these problem solving processes draws not only upon problem solvers' knowledge bases, but also their reasoning skills. For example, in understanding a problem situation, the problem solver may need to distinguish between facts and opinion. In formulating a solution, the problem solver may need to identify relationships between variables. In selecting a strategy, the problem solver may need to consider cause and effect. In communicating the results, the problem solver may need to organise information in a logical manner. These activities often require analytic reasoning, quantitative reasoning, analogical reasoning and combinatorial reasoning skills. These reasoning skills form the core of problem solving competencies.

Box 4.1 ■ TYPES OF REASONING SKILLS

Analytic reasoning is characterised by situations where the learner must apply principles from formal logic in determining necessary and sufficient conditions, or in determining if implication of causality occurs among the constraints and conditions provided in the problem stimulus.

Quantitative reasoning is characterised by situations where the learner must apply properties and procedures related to number sense and number operations from the discipline of mathematics to solve the given problem.

Analogical reasoning is characterised by situations where the learner must solve a problem with a context similar to a problem the learner is familiar with, or includes a problem base which the learner has solved in the past. The parameters or the context in the new stimulus material is changed, but the driving factors or causal mechanism is the same. The learner should be able to solve the new problem by interpreting it in light of past experience with the analogous situation.

Combinatorial reasoning is characterised by situations where the learner must examine a variety of factors, consider all combinations in which they can appear, evaluate each of these individual combinations relative to some objective constraint and then select from or rank order the combinations.

Thus, the act of problem solving is the amalgam of many different cognitive processes that are orchestrated to achieve a certain goal that could not be reached, at least obviously, by simply applying a well-known procedure, process, routine or algorithm from a single subject area. Problem solving competence can be described in terms of students' abilities to create and monitor a number of processes within a certain range of tasks and situations. Problem solving assessment strives to identify the processes used in a variety of situations and content areas and to describe and quantify, where possible, the quality of the products of the students' work.

The elements of the PISA 2003 assessment of problem solving are shown in Figure 4.1. The relationships illustrate how such an assessment draws both on context and content knowledge from various fields, as well as on competencies found in the content areas and in problem solving as a domain in itself.

Figure 4.1 ■ **Visualisation of the key components of problem solving framework**

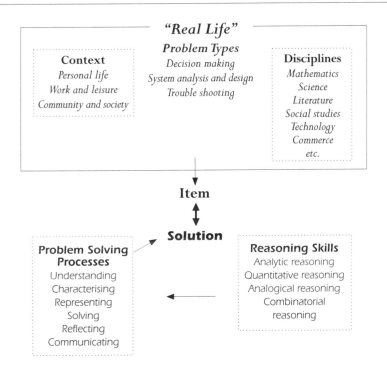

Problem types

For cross-disciplinary problem solving assessment in PISA 2003, it was decided to limit the assessment of student capabilities to three broad areas of problem solving, which will be referred to as "problem-types". These three problem types are: *decision making*, *system analysis and design*, and *trouble shooting*.

Decision making, *system analysis and design*, and *trouble shooting* are generic problem solving structures that capture important aspects of the everyday, real-life, analytical reasoning that we would like to assess in the assessment programme. They provide an alternative to the content domains of the reading, mathematical and scientific literacy assessments. In those assessments, there is a well-defined knowledge domain that provides the needed structure to bound the assessment. In testing problem solving, the emphasis is on process rather than on domain knowledge. However, processes cannot be assessed without being attached to some kind of structure. The three proposed problem types provide the generic structures within which problem solving processes can be assessed.

Decision making

Decision making problems require students to understand a situation involving a number of alternatives and constraints, and to make a decision that satisfies the constraints. For example, in Problem Solving Unit 1: Say No To Pain, students are asked to decide which of a selection of pain killers is the most suitable one, considering the patient's age, symptoms and other medical conditions.

Decision making tasks such as the above typically involve comprehending the information given and the demands of the task, identifying the relevant features or constraints that must be met, creating a representation of the problem or alternatives, making a decision that meets the constraints, checking to see that the solution meets the constraints and then communicating or justifying the decision. In *decision making* tasks of this type, the student needs to select an alternative from a number of given ones. In doing this, the student must usually combine information from a number of diverse sources (combinatorial reasoning) and select the best solution.

A *decision making* problem will be more difficult if it is more complex. For example, the decision to buy a car becomes more difficult when the amount of information to be analyzed increases, the information involves a number of different representations that must be linked, or a greater number of constraints must be attended to. Some students may be able to deal with easy *decision making* tasks but fail when the complexity of a task increases.

When the complexity of a *decision making* task is high, external representations can become very useful. In Problem Solving Unit 1: Say No to Pain, such a representation is already constructed, in the form of a table. For other *decision making* tasks, students may be required to create such representations, in the form of tables, diagrams, graphs, etc. Students' abilities to create relevant representations or to apply a given representation, such as making or interpreting a graph, are factors in their performances on *decision making* tasks. Once a representation is constructed or applied, the student must select, relate and compare the information as organised by the representation and choose the best alternative.

Problem Solving Unit 1
SAY NO TO PAIN

It is not easy to choose the right pain killer for occasional aches and pains, as there are so many different brands of pain killers on the market, all claiming to be the right one for you.

The Care Medical group provides the following information about 4 different painkillers:

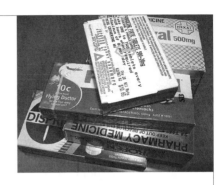

Pain killer Name	Description	For the Relief of Symptoms	Dosage	Caution Notes
Aquaspirin	100% dissolvable aspirin tablet. Good for people who cannot face taking pills.	Headache; Muscle pain; Dental pain; Back pain; Sore throat; Reduce inflammation and fever.	**Adult and children over 12 years of age**: 1 to 2 tablets dissolved in half a glass of water every 4 hours as needed. Do not exceed 8 tablets in 24 hours. **Children under 12 years of age**: Do not administer Aquaspirin to children under 12 years of age.	Prolonged use could be harmful. Should not be taken by a person on a low sodium diet.
Paracem	100% paracetamol. Suitable for breastfeeding mothers and asthmatics. Does not cause stomach irritations like aspirin.	Headache; Backache; Toothache; Muscular pain; Arthritis; Reduce fever.	**Adult and children over 12 years of age**: 1 to 2 tablets every 4 hours as needed. **Children under 12 years of age**: 0.5 to 1 tablet every 4 hours as needed.	Prolonged use could be harmful.
NoAx	Each tablet contains 25mg of Diclofenac Potassium. Suitable for the relief of acute, painful and inflammatory conditions. Pain relief is usually within 15 to 30 minutes.	Bruises; Neck pain; Back pain, Sprains and strains; Migraine; Pain after surgery.	**Adult and children over 14 years of age**: 1 to 2 tablets every 8 hours. Do not exceed 6 tablets a day. **Children 14 years and under**: Children 14 years and under should not take NoAx.	Do not take NoAx on an empty stomach. Check with your doctor if you suffer from asthma, or if you are taking any other medication. Possible side-effects: dizziness, swelling of feet.
Reliefen	Each tablet contains 200mg of ibuprofen. It is gentler on the stomach than aspirin.	Headache; Muscle & rheumatic pain; Dental pain; Cold symptoms; Backache; Reduce fever & inflammation.	**Adult and children over 12 years of age**: 1 to 2 tablets every 4 - 6 hours. Do not exceed 6 tablets in 24 hours. **Children 12 years and under**: Reliefen is not suitable for children 12 years and under.	If you suffer from asthma, kidney disorder, are allergic to aspirin or are pregnant, you should consult your doctor before taking Reliefen.

Problem Solving Example 1.1

From the information given, rank the four pain killers from the weakest to the strongest. (Write the numbers 1 to 4 in the boxes, with 4 as the strongest).

☐ Aquaspirin

☐ Paracem

☐ NoAx

☐ Reliefen

Scoring

Full credit

Code 1: Answers that present 2, 1, 4, 3 in that order.

No credit

Code 0: Other responses.

Problem Solving Example 1.2

Identify **two** pain killers that may cause more stomach irritation than the other two.

A. Aquaspirin

B. Paracem

C. NoAx

D. Reliefen

Scoring

Full credit

Code 1: Answers that indicate A and C as the two pain killers that may cause stomach irritation.

No credit

Code 0: Other responses.

Problem Solving Example 1.3

Michael's mother took some Reliefen tablets for a cold and headache. She took two tablets at 8 am, one tablet at 1 pm and two tablets at 6 pm. Before going to bed at 11 pm, how many tablets could she take, according to the dosage instructions?

Scoring

Full credit

Code 1: Answers that specify "one tablet", so that the total does not exceed six tablets within 24 hours.

No credit

Code 0: Other answers.

Problem Solving Example 1.4

Choose the pain killer most suitable for each of the following patients, based on the information given.

PATIENT	CIRCLE THE MOST SUITABLE PAIN KILLER
Emma, a 10-year-old child with a cold and fever.	Aquaspirin/Paracem/NoAx/Reliefen
George, a 13-year-old asthmatic boy with a sprained ankle, needing a pain killer to reduce pain and inflammation.	Aquaspirin/Paracem/NoAx/Reliefen
William, a 45-year old machine operator, needing a long-lasting pain killer for back pain that he can take each day.	Aquaspirin/Paracem/NoAx/Reliefen
Susan, a breastfeeding mother, suffering from a headache.	Aquaspirin/Paracem/NoAx/Reliefen

Scoring

Full credit

Code 1: Answers that specify Paracem, Aquaspirin, Reliefen, Paracem, in that order:

No credit

Code 0: Any other combination of answers.

After making a decision, students must be able to evaluate, justify and communicate this decision to an outside audience. The ability to justify and communicate a problem solution is an important aspect of students' *decision making* capabilities.

To summarise, *decision making* tasks require understanding the given information, identifying the relevant alternatives and the constraints involved, constructing or applying external representations, selecting the best solution from a set of given alternatives and evaluating, justifying or communicating the decision.

System analysis and design

System analysis and design problems require a student to analyse a complex situation in order to understand its logic and/or to design a system that works and achieves certain goals, given information about the relationships among features of the problem context. For example, in Problem Solving Unit 2: Managing CD Sales, the student is asked to analyse a record keeping system for managing CD sales in a music store.

A *system analysis and design* problem is different from a *decision making* problem in at least two critical aspects: *i)* the student is asked to analyse a system or design a solution to a problem rather than to select one of a set of alternatives; and *ii)* the situation described usually consists of a complex system of interrelated variables, where one variable influences others and the solution is not always clear-cut. In other words, *system analysis and design* problems are characterised by the dynamic nature of the relationships among the variables involved and the possible non-uniqueness of the solution. These types of problems occur often in disciplines such as economics or environmental sciences. In *decision making* tasks, the variables typically do not interact in such complex ways, the constraints are more clear-cut and the decisions are easier to justify.

System analysis and design tasks usually require identifying related variables and finding out how they will interact. In such problem settings, students must be able to analyse complex situations and determine the relationships defining the systems, or to design a system that satisfies the given relationships and achieves the relevant goals. The ability to evaluate, justify and communicate a solution to a *system analysis and design* problem is also an integral part of the entire process.

As was seen in examining *decision making* problems, the difficulty of a *system analysis and design* problem is also affected by its complexity. The more complex a situation (in terms of the number of variables, but also in terms of their interrelations), the greater the difficulty of the problem solving task. The creation of a representation or the application of a given or known representation is a necessary part of the process of solving the problem.

In Problem Solving Unit 2: Managing CD Sales, the student is asked to identify variables that are relevant for CD sales and to analyse the relationships among them to determine the best way to organise information. This task also requires students to work out methods of information retrieval using logical reasoning.

Problem Solving Unit 2
MANAGING CD SALES

The Fine Melody CD store is developing a system for keeping records of music CDs sold by the store. They prepared two record sheets on the computer as shown below:

Record Sheet 1: Attributes of each CD (One line per CD)

CD Serial ID Number	Title of CD	CD Company
14339	Spring Carnival	NAXA
10292	Hits of the '90s	FineStudio
00551	Arias for Opera Lovers	DigiRec

Record Sheet 2: Attributes of each track on CD (One line per track)

CD Serial ID Number	Track number	Track Name
14339	1	Spring Fever
14339	2	Leap into Spring
14339	3	Midnight Rhythm
10292	1	Best Dance in Town

Problem Solving Example 2.1

Which record sheet (1 or 2) should each of the following attributes be added to?

ATTRIBUTE	EXAMPLE ENTRIES	CIRCLE "RECORD SHEET 1" OR "RECORD SHEET 2"
ARTIST/BAND/ ORCHESTRA	Faye Weber; Berlin Philharmonic	Record Sheet 1/Record Sheet 2
PRICE OF CD	15 zeds; 25 zeds for a set of two.	Record Sheet 1/Record Sheet 2
STOCK STATUS	On order; In stock	Record Sheet 1/Record Sheet 2
COMPOSER	Warren Jones; Li Yuan	Record Sheet 1/Record Sheet 2

Scoring

Full credit

Code 1: Answers that specify Record Sheet 2, Record Sheet 1, Record Sheet 1, Record Sheet 2, in that order.

No credit

Code 0: Any other combination of answers.

Problem Solving Example 2.2

Add **two** attributes for Record Sheet 1, and **two** attributes for Record Sheet 2, with example entries. Do not include attributes that have already been mentioned.

Scoring

List of attributes for Record Sheet 1:

> • copyright/release year for CD, *e.g.*, ©1998.
>
> • total CD playing time, *e.g.*, 78 minutes.
>
> • CD categories: classical, popular, alternative.

List of attributes for Record Sheet 2:

> • track playing time, *e.g.*, 5'32".
>
> • year/place of recording, *e.g.*, March 1998, Prague.
>
> • lyric writer, *e.g.*, Sharon Green.

Full credit

Code 2: Answers that include:

> • two attributes for Record Sheet 1 from the above list of attributes.
> AND
>
> • two attributes for Record Sheet 2 from the above list of attributes.

Partial credit

Code 1: Answers that are incomplete, such as mentioning:

> • only two attributes for Record Sheet 1
> OR
>
> • only two attributes for Record Sheet 2
> OR
>
> • one attribute for Record Sheet 1 and one attribute for Record Sheet 2;
> OR
>
> • two attributes for each Record but with no example entries.

No credit

Code 0: Other answers.

Problem Solving Example 2.3

The record keeping system allows users to search for particular CDs. The following shows how search commands are written, using brackets ( ) and the key words: "AND" and "OR":

(1) To find all CDs under 15 zeds with recordings made by vocalist Irena Emile, write the following search command:

(Price < 15) AND (Artist=Irena Emile).

(2) To find all CDs with recordings of Beethoven's Fifth Symphony recorded by the Boston or Chicago Symphony Orchestras, write the following search command:

(Track name=Beethoven's Fifth Symphony) AND (Orchestra=Boston OR Chicago).

Write a search command to find all of the CDs produced by the recording companies NAXA or DigiRec of the recordings of the song "Last Night I Had a Dream".

Scoring

Full credit

Code 1:   Answers that include:

> (Track=Last Night I Had a Dream) AND (Company=NAXA OR DigiRec).
>
> Note that the emphasis is on the placement of AND, OR and the brackets. The actual texts and order of the brackets are not important. The exact form of the key words such as "track" and "company" is not important. Thus, "title" is acceptable instead of "track name", "producer" instead of "company", etc.

No credit

Code 0:   Other answers.

Evaluation, justification and communication of a solution are very important parts of the problem solving process in a *system analysis and design* task. The solution to such a task is generally not unique or obvious and there are possible advantages and disadvantages associated with each possible solution.

To summarise, a *systems analysis and design* task usually requires understanding the complex relationships among a number of interdependent variables, identifying their critical features, creating or applying a given representation, analysing a complex situation or designing a system so that certain goals are achieved. It also normally involves a good deal of checking and evaluating as the student moves through the various steps along the way to an analysis or design.

Trouble shooting

Trouble shooting problems require a student to comprehend the main features of a system and to diagnose a faulty, or under-performing, feature of the system or mechanism. For example, in Problem Solving Unit 3: Bicycle Pump, Jane is asked to find out why air is not coming out of her bicycle tyre pump. Despite the fact that she repeatedly pulled up and pushed down on the handle-piston assembly of the pump, no air was pumped out. Jane will not be able to make her diagnosis unless she understands how the bicycle tyre pump works and, more specifically, the function of the inner and outer valves and the piston in transferring air from outside of the pump into the bicycle tyre attached to the pump hose.

Trouble shooting tasks can be clearly distinguished from *decision making* and *system analysis and design* tasks. *Trouble shooting* problems involve neither selecting the best of a set of given options, nor the design of a system to fit a given set of requirements. Rather, *trouble shooting* tasks require the understanding of the logic of a causal mechanism, such as the workings of a physical system or a procedure. For example, a retail company needs to find the causes for their declining sales figures or a computer programmer needs to find the error in a program.

Despite the differences in the structures of the three problem types, the student solving a *trouble shooting* task must also understand how the device or procedure works (*i.e.*, understand the mechanism), identify the critical features for the diagnosis of the specific problem he or she is asked to solve, create or apply the relevant representations, diagnose the problem, propose a solution and, when the situation requires it, execute the solution.

Representation is very important in *trouble shooting* problems because they often require the integration of verbal and pictorial information. In Problem Solving Unit 3: Bicycle Pump, Jane must integrate the pictorial and verbal information to arrive at an understanding of the mechanism of the pump. In other situations, the student may need to create a pictorial representation out of a verbal description or describe verbally a drawing that demonstrates how a device works. The ability to move flexibly from one representation to another is an important aspect of problem solving that is often involved in *trouble shooting* problems. Finally, evaluation, justification and communication are as important in *trouble shooting* problems as in the other problem types. For example, in Problem Solving Example 3.2, reasons have to be given to support claims.

To summarise, *trouble shooting* tasks involve diagnosing, proposing a solution and, at times, executing this solution. The tasks require the student to understand how a device or procedure works, to identify the relevant features for the task at hand and to create a representation or apply a given representation.

Problem Solving Unit 3
BICYCLE PUMP

Jane had some trouble with her bicycle tyre pump yesterday. She repeatedly pulled up and pushed down on the handle of the pump, but no air came out of the hose. She wanted to find out what was wrong, so she looked in the box where the pump was kept and found a piece of paper with the following information on it.

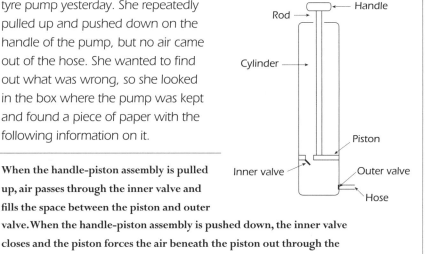

Bicycle tyre pump

When the handle-piston assembly is pulled up, air passes through the inner valve and fills the space between the piston and outer valve. When the handle-piston assembly is pushed down, the inner valve closes and the piston forces the air beneath the piston out through the outer valve.

Problem Solving Example 3.1

Explain how the movement of the valves enables the operation of the bicycle pump when the handle-piston assembly is in different positions.

Scoring

Full credit

Code 2: Answers that describe what happens with BOTH movements of the handle-piston assembly.

- When the handle-piston assembly is pushed down, the inner valve closes and the outer valve opens.

AND

- When the handle-piston assembly is pulled up, the inner valve opens and the outer valve closes.

Partial credit

Code 1: Answers that describe what happens with the movement of the handle-piston assembly in one direction only.

- When the handle-piston assembly is pushed down, the inner valve closes and the outer valve opens.

OR

- When the handle-piston assembly is pulled up, the inner valve opens and the outer valve closes.

No credit

Code 0: Other answers.

Problem Solving Example 3.2

Identify two possible reasons that would result in no air coming from the hose. Give an argument supporting the possibility of each of your reasons.

Scoring

Possible reasons and explanations:

- inner valve is stuck closed and thus no air can come into the cylinder beneath the piston;
- outer valve is stuck closed and does not allow air to get out of the hose;
- piston is worn and thus there is no compression to force air to the hose;
- there is a leak in the cylinder wall below the piston, defeating compression;
- there is a leak in the hose, allowing air to escape;
- no air intake to cylinder.

Full credit

Code 2: Answers that mention TWO reasons with explanations.

Partial credit

Code 1: Answers that mention only ONE reason with an explanation.

No credit

Code 0: Other answers.

Problem solving processes

The development of a framework for problem solving requires the processes involved in student work on problem solving to be identified. This is not easy, as the ways in which various individuals solve problems do not fit into a standard format. The processes proposed below are based on the cognitive analysis of the three problem types described earlier, guided by the work on problem solving and reasoning of cognitive psychologists (*e.g.*, Mayer & Wittrock, 1996; Bransford et al, 1999; Baxter & Glaser, 1997; Vosniadou & Ortony, 1989), as well as by the seminal work of Polya (1945). The model proposed consists of processes that provide an organisational structure for examining student work and organising the problem solving assessment tasks. Note that no assumption is made that these processes are either hierarchical or necessary for the solution of any particular problem. As individuals confront, structure, represent and solve problems in a dynamic, real-time fashion, they may move to a solution in a way that transcends the narrow linearity of the present model. Indeed, most of the information about the functioning of the human cognitive system now supports the view that it is a parallel rather than a linear information processing system.

- *Understanding the problem.* This includes how students understand a text, a diagram, a formula or a table and draw inferences from it; relate information from various sources; demonstrate understanding of relevant concepts; and use information from their background knowledge to understand the information given.

- *Characterising the problem.* This includes how students identify the variables in the problem and their interrelationships; decide which variables are relevant and irrelevant; construct hypotheses; and retrieve, organise, consider and critically evaluate contextual information.

- *Representing the problem.* This includes how students construct tabular, graphical, symbolic or verbal representations, or how they apply a given external representation to the solution of the problem; and how they shift between representational formats.

- *Solving the problem.* This includes making a decision (in the case of *decision making*); analysing a system or designing a system to meet certain goals (in the case of *system analysis and design*), or diagnosing and proposing a solution (in the case of *trouble shooting*).

- *Reflecting on the solution.* This includes how students examine their solutions and look for additional information or clarification; evaluate their solutions from different perspectives in an attempt to restructure the solutions and make them more socially or technically acceptable; and justify their solutions.

- *Communicating the problem solution.* This includes how students select appropriate media and representations to express and communicate their solutions to an outside audience.

Summary of problem types

The entries of Table 4.1 summarise the basic features of the three problem types in terms of the goal, the problem solving process involved and the source of increasing complexity associated with the problems.

Situations

The assessment of problem solving in OECD/PISA should require students to apply their knowledge and skills in some new way; to transfer their capacities from one setting to another; and to use their knowledge in handling *decision making*, *system analysis and design* and *trouble shooting* problems. As such, the cross-disciplinary problem solving work will, in many cases, approach the notion of "life skills". The problems will usually be embedded in real-life settings associated with personal life, work and leisure, or community and society.

LOCATING PROBLEM SOLVING WITHIN PISA 2003

While reading, mathematics and science are three major content domains in every education system, they do not provide all of the skills students need in preparation for adult life. An examination of the entering knowledge and skills expected of citizens and members of the workforce in the 21st century indicates that these expectations are changing as rapidly as advances in technology. As various forms of technology have replaced forms of manual labour, new knowledge and skills have supplanted more traditional content as entry expectations to adult life and work. The OECD/PISA assessments must measure

Table 4.1 ■ **Facets of problem solving types**

	Decision making	System analysis and design	Trouble shooting
Goal	Choosing among alternatives under constraints	Identifying the relationships between parts of a system and/or designing a system to express the relationships between parts	Diagnosing and correcting a faulty or under-performing system or mechanism
Processes involved	Understanding a situation where there exist several alternatives and constraints and a specified task	Understanding the information that characterises a given system and requirements associated with a specified task	Understanding the main features of a system or mechanism and its malfunctioning, and the demands of a specific task
	Identifying relevant constraints	Identifying relevant parts of the system	Identifying causally related variables
	Representing the possible alternatives	Representing the relationships among parts of the system	Representing the functioning of the system
	Making a decision amongst alternatives	Analysing or designing a system that captures the relationships between the parts	Diagnosing the malfunctioning of the system and/or proposing a solution
	Checking and evaluating the decision	Checking and evaluating the analysis or the design of the system	Checking and evaluating the diagnosis and solution
	Communicating or justifying the decision	Communicating the analysis or justifying the proposed design	Communicating or justifying the diagnosis and the solution
Possible sources of complexity	Number of constraints	Number of inter-related variables and nature of relationships	Number of inter-related parts to the system or mechanism and the ways in which these parts interact
	Number and type of representations used (verbal, pictorial, numerical)	Number and type of representations used (verbal, pictorial, numerical)	Number and type of representations used (verbal, pictorial, numerical)

students' capabilities to adapt to change and to solve problems that require emerging key competencies.

Key competencies

The development of lists of skills or key competencies has been a central goal of several OECD activities, most visibly in the DeSeCo Project (Rychen & Salganik, 2000). This work found that key competencies are multifunctional and multidimensional in nature, and allow one to traverse domains and deal with higher orders of mental complexity. Key competencies enable individuals to deal with complex situations in active and reflective ways. In particular, they assist individuals in moving from dualistic views of their surroundings or issues to vantage points that reveal multiple, and sometime conflicting, interpretations of contexts and events. As such, they call on multiple mental processes. Although not always part of the OECD/PISA assessments, the processes listed in the DeSeCo report include:

- recognising and analysing patterns, establishing analogies between experienced situations and new ones (*coping with complexity*);

- perceiving situations, discriminating between relevant and irrelevant features (*perceptive dimension*);

- choosing appropriate means to reach given ends, appreciating various possibilities offered, making judgements and applying them (*normative dimension*);

- developing social orientation, trusting other people, listening and understanding others' positions (*co-operative dimension*);

- making sense of what happens in life to oneself and others, seeing and describing the world and one's real and desirable place in it (*narrative dimension*).

An appraisal of these processes shows that problem solving, viewed as a cross-disciplinary activity, is at the heart of the key competencies. The recognition, abstraction, generalisation and evaluation of patterns and the development of associated plans of action based on these processes are a core part of what problem solving adds in educational, vocational and professional decision making. Perceiving situations within complex contexts, and delineating the relevant features and constraints, are central to analysing systems and structures and to developing plans of action to confront problems in all forms of human activity. Choosing appropriate means to reach specified or desired ends is what problem solving adds to confronting difficulties encountered in life or in one's work.

Problem solving in employment trends and skills demand

As today's 15-year-olds will enter the work force within ten years, it is important, in evaluating their preparedness for life, to identify characteristics of the labour market they will encounter. Studies and surveys of employment trends and related skill demands indicate significant changes have occurred in the labour market over the past 20 years (ILO, 1998; OECD, 2001b).

Rapid technological advances and globalisation in business and industry have resulted in increased demands for highly-skilled professionals and technicians. These demands, in turn, have resulted in calls for education reform, both in formal schooling and in workplace training. In the United States, the Secretary's Commission on Achieving Necessary Skills (SCANS) report (U.S. Department of Labor, 1991) proposed a way for schools to conceive of needed knowledge and skills beyond the traditional academic disciplines. The SCANS framework consists of a three-part foundation accompanied by five general competencies (Stern, 1999). The skills foundation consists of:

- *basic skills*: reading, writing, arithmetic and mathematics, listening and speaking;

- *thinking skills*: creative thinking, decision making, problem solving, seeing things in the mind's eye, knowing how to learn and reasoning;

- *personal qualities*: responsibility, self-esteem, sociability, self-management and integrity/honesty.

The associated competencies include:

- *resources*: managing time, money, materials, facilities and human resources;

- *interpersonal*: participating on teams, assisting in teaching others, serving clients/customers, exercising leadership, negotiating and working with diversity;

- *information*: acquiring and evaluating, organising and maintaining, interpreting and communicating and using computers to process information;

- *systems*: understanding systems, monitoring and correcting performance, and improving or designing systems;

- *technology*: selecting technology, applying technology to tasks, and maintaining and troubleshooting equipment.

Thus, while the major academic subjects of reading, writing and mathematics are prominent in the SCANS basic skills strand, the developers of the SCANS report, like those of the DeSeCo report, have separated out problem solving and critical reasoning skills as a separate domain of study. This does not indicate a lack of problem solving activity or critical thinking in reading, mathematics and science. What it indicates is that there is an emerging and widespread belief that problem solving stands as a separate and well-recognised domain of human activity that is separate from the contributions of the disciplinary domains.

The SCANS and DeSeCo reports are but two examples of analyses of the knowledge and skills demanded by current and emerging conceptions of work force needs. Numerous other analyses have also provided similar pictures of the generic and work-related skills today's students will need. McCurry (2002) has provided an analysis of such reports. It shows that, apart from the knowledge and skills associated with traditional academic domains, problem solving or general thinking skills is an identified core competency for life and work in the world of tomorrow.

Contrasting PISA problem solving with the literacy domains

The assessment of cross-disciplinary problem solving in PISA 2003 differs from studies of problem solving in the three PISA literacy assessments and in extant psychological studies in several important respects. First, in OECD/PISA assessments of reading, mathematical and scientific literacy, problem solving is used to assess knowledge and understanding in the individual domains, while in OECD/PISA problem solving, the emphasis is on problem solving processes themselves. Secondly, OECD/PISA problem solving differs from the assessments in the literacy domains in that it emphasises the integration of information from different discipline areas, rather than drawing mainly on one domain of knowledge. Finally, the OECD/PISA assessments are different in the openness of their solutions and the complexity of the critical reasoning skills involved.

In its attempt to measure problem solving, the OECD/PISA assessment shares the project approach and focus on analytic reasoning with the International Survey of Adults (ISA) and some portions of the German national option from PISA 2000. On the other hand, the OECD/PISA assessment focuses on only three defined problem types, allowing for a clearer and deeper assessment of certain processes that students employ in these approaches. Perhaps most importantly, OECD/PISA differs from other large-scale educational assessment studies in that it is not curriculum based. Rather, OECD/PISA sets out to assess 15-year-old students' preparedness for life. As such, while the reading, mathematics and science frameworks all stress the literacy viewpoint and specify the roles that key concepts and skills in these domains play in preparing students for adult life, OECD/PISA problem solving focuses on the generic problem solving and reasoning skills that transcend academic domains.

Assessing processes rather than knowledge

As OECD/PISA problem solving focuses on generic reasoning and problem solving processes, it is important to recognise that problem solving is not a subject matter domain. Rather, problem solving is about the application of the processes people use in confronting problem situations (NCTM, 2000). Thus, OECD/PISA problem solving examines student work by concentrating on how students come to:

- understand the nature of a problem;
- characterise the problem by identifying variables and relationships inherent in the problem;
- select and adjust representations of the problem;
- solve the problem;
- reflect on the solution of a problem;
- communicate the solution of a problem.

Focusing on these processes rather than simply on final solutions permits an understanding of how people approach solving problems. Mayer (1985) notes that this information-processing approach to examining problem solving is based on task analysis. As such, it provides an independent description of what problem solving contributes beyond just a score on a test. Understanding the processes involved can also help teachers to prepare instructional activities in teaching problem solving.

Problem solving types

As noted earlier, the three problem types used in the PISA 2003 assessment are *decision making*, *system analysis and design*, and *trouble shooting*. These problem types fit in well with both the SCANS and DeSeCo recommendations. The main reason for restricting the number of problem solving types is the limited time available for the assessment of problem solving. While it would be possible to select problem solving tasks from an extremely broad range of task demands, to identify likely strategies and to develop related contexts for setting the problems it was decided to limit the types and demands of the problems studied.

Within the three PISA problem solving types, many tasks involve problems dealing with scheduling, allocating resources, tracing the causes of problems, evaluating and organising information, and finding best options. While none of the tasks involves in-depth knowledge of reading, mathematics and science, they all involve logical thinking and analytical reasoning. These tasks do not belong to the reading, mathematics or science domains, but rather focus on the important foundational problem solving skills identified by the reports summarised earlier.

In order to adequately measure the cross-disciplinary aspects of problem solving, it is important that:

- the assessment focuses as heavily on the processes students use in solving problems as it does on the correctness of the solutions offered;

- domain-specific problem solving competencies related to the OECD/PISA literacy domains are included in the expectations, but that the problems employed to assess problem solving as a cross-disciplinary competency generally reach beyond a single domain by making connections to both non-subject area aspects of the curricular fields and by crossing subject matter curricular boundaries;

- cross-disciplinary problem solving competencies should be assessed by tasks that extend subject area measures in terms of content (focusing on real-life situations calling for transfer of curricular learning) and setting (focusing on complex, dynamic, real-life environments as well as reasoning tasks).

It is clear that cross-disciplinary problem solving forms an integral part of the skills demand for the current and future workforce and that the OECD/PISA problem solving component fills some gaps in assessing students' preparedness for life over and above the more academic domains. The current problem solving framework does not, however, cover all areas of problem solving: for example, interpersonal and group problem solving are regarded as important by many employers.

ASSESSMENT CHARACTERISTICS

Accessibility and equity

The assessment should be accessible to students regardless of the educational programmes in the participating countries. This means that the item can be understood and addressed by 15-year-old students regardless of the curriculum in which they are enrolled. Items should be developed in different representational modes (graph, table, words, symbols, pictures, etc.) that are easily interpretable by *all* students. Further, it is assumed that care will be taken that other sources of bias are avoided in the design and construction of the items. For example, excessively technical vocabulary, difficult reading level/vocabulary and items calling for specific personal life experiences should be avoided.

Calculators

An assessment of problem solving does not focus on students' ability to perform calculations. All students participating in the OECD/PISA problem solving assessment should therefore be allowed to use any hand calculators they routinely use in their classroom environments. The decision on whether or not to use calculators should rest with the individual students, based on their knowledge of when a calculator is appropriate and how it might add to the solution of a problem. No item should be constructed so that its solution is dependent solely on whether a calculator is used or not, or is of such a length that students not using a calculator would be severely disadvantaged in performing any calculations required.

ITEM TYPES

In previous large-scale assessments of problem solving, the types of items used have been multiple-choice, true-false or short response. These item types were used because they were viewed as contributing to higher reliability, providing more objectivity, reducing scoring costs and easing administration requirements when compared to assessments involving student constructed responses. However, to adequately ascertain students' abilities to reason, solve problems and communicate the results of such activities, more extensive records of their work are needed. Further, to adequately measure and describe students' work, it is important to be able to examine a variety of types of students' thinking in problem-related settings. Hence, a wider variety of item types is needed for the PISA 2003 cross-disciplinary problem solving assessment. In addition to multiple-choice items, the assessment will contain both closed and open constructed-response items. Each of these item types is described below.

Multiple-choice items

Multiple-choice items are appropriate for quickly and inexpensively determining whether students have mastered certain skills, knowledge or information gathering abilities. Well-designed multiple-choice items can measure student knowledge and

understanding, as well as students' selection and application of problem solving strategies. They can be designed to reach beyond the ability of students to "plug-in" alternatives or eliminate choices to determine a correct answer. However, multiple-choice items are somewhat limited in their ability to ascertain the full breadth and depth of a student's problem solving capabilities in many contexts.

Multiple-choice items in the OECD/PISA problem solving assessment should:

- not be answerable by simply plugging in values or by estimating measurements or size comparisons in the graphics supplied by the item;

- have distracters/alternatives designed to ascertain how students do or do not cope with a situation proposed in an item and to provide information about their thought processes, not to trick them into common error patterns;

- be used when an alternative item type would require students to draw a graph or construct a figure that would be complicated or time-consuming.

Closed constructed-response items

Closed constructed-response items allow examiners to assess higher-order goals and more complex processes in a controlled response format. Closed constructed-response items are similar to multiple-choice items, but students are asked to produce a response that can be easily judged to be either correct or incorrect. Guessing is less of a concern with closed constructed-response items, and they allow examiners to see what students can produce in a setting that does not call for "expert" marking and where partial credit is not an issue.

Closed constructed-response items on the OECD/PISA problem solving assessment should:

- be used when it is important to see that students can produce the answer to the item on their own;

- state explicitly what students need to do in responding;

- involve a limited range of responses in order that they can be quickly marked with a high degree of reliability.

Open constructed-response items

Open constructed-response items allow examiners to ascertain what students can produce based on their own understanding of an item and what students can communicate about how they solved the item. Short open constructed-response items require students to give brief answers: numerical results, the correct name or classification for a group of objects, an example of a given concept, etc.

Short open constructed-response items on the OECD/PISA problem solving assessment should:

- be used when it is important to see that students can produce the answer to the item on their own;

- state explicitly what students needs to do in responding;

- allow examination of the degree to which students understand the problem.

Long open constructed-response items require students to show more complete evidence of their work or to show that they have used more complex thought processes in solving a problem. In either case, students are expected to clearly communicate their decision-making processes in the context of the problem (*e.g.*, through writing, pictures, diagrams, or well-ordered steps).

Open constructed-response items on the OECD/PISA problem solving assessment should:

- ask students to show integration of information or concepts, along with the way in which these lead to the solution of the problem proposed;

- tap multiple areas of understanding and require their connection in the students' responses.

- be used when the situation requires multiple steps to a solution and has several different components;

- require students to explain or justify the work produced;

- be amenable to rubric scoring in order that trained markers can mark the items efficiently and reliably.

Groups or units of items

In order to support a student's deep engagement with some problems (and possibly combat response motivation difficulties), the majority of items in the problem solving assessment should be developed in groups or units, about themes or project-based situations. Such units should contain collections of two or more items, often involving different representations or measured by different item types, which are related either by a shared topic focus or by a common context. In either instance, the items in the units should be independent, at least to the extent that a correct answer to one item in the set is not required in order to get a subsequent item correct.

Marking guides

Marking guides or rubrics for evaluating student responses to items should be constructed within a general framework that values the major aspects of problem solving. Such rubrics should allow the recognition of student work attaining the levels of:

- understanding the information given;

- identifying or characterising the critical features and their interrelationships;

- constructing or applying a representation of the problem;

- solving the problem;

- checking, evaluating or justifying aspects of the problem;

- communicating the problem solution.

In such rubrics, the highest level of scoring should reflect a complete understanding of the problem, require a correct solution, reward thought that shows considerable insight, and reflect work that is clear, appropriate and fully developed. Such responses should be logically sound, clearly written and contain no errors. Any examples given should be well chosen and fully developed.

At a slightly lower score level, one might encounter work that demonstrates a clear understanding of the problem, shows some insight and provides an acceptable approach, but still contains minor weaknesses in its development. Examples are provided, but they may not be fully developed.

At an even lower level, one may see work that contains evidence of an understanding of the problem at a conceptual level, evidenced by the logical approach taken or representation chosen. However, on the whole, such a response is not well developed. While there may be serious logical errors or flaws in the reasoning, the response does contain some correct work. The examples provided may be incorrect or incomplete.

Finally, there would be a no credit level for coding completely incorrect or irrelevant responses. Within the scoring at this level, some allowance should be made for distinguishing between students who attempt a given problem and those who submit a blank response. The latter may signal either lack of time or a motivational problem.

It should be noted that not every item will elicit all of the three positive credit levels described above, but collectively for the problem solving test, there will be items tapping into different levels of student performance.

Double-digit scoring

In addition to scoring the student responses for correctness, the marking guides or rubrics should provide a basis for scoring the items for the strategies employed by students in solving a given problem, or for showing the misconceptions that prevented students from reaching a correct solution. This form of scoring is useful in attempting to grasp the nature of student thinking and the degree to which students have some command of higher-order thinking skills. Such scoring can be accomplished via the use of the dual coding scoring methods used in both the TIMSS and PISA 2000 assessments. This approach employs a two-digit code in scoring the items. The first digit of the code indicates whether the student receives (full or partial) credit, provided incorrect work, wrote unintelligible work or left the response area blank. The second digit of the code provides information on the type of approach that the student used if the item was worked correctly. If the student did not receive any credit, the second digit could provide information on the error patterns or misconceptions that characterise the student work.

General structure of the assessment

The cross-disciplinary problem solving assessment will consist of two 30-minute clusters of units of items. The three problem types (*decision making*, *system analysis and design*, and *trouble shooting*) are represented, respectively, in the ratio of 2:2:1.

Each cluster has items grouped into four or five different units. There are about 50 per cent single marker items (multiple-choice and closed constructed-response items) and about 50 per cent items requiring multiple markers (open constructed-response items). Each unit should have at least one item that requires students to solve or evaluate a solution strategy for the focus problem of the unit.

The degree of explicitness of the information for the tasks can vary. Some tasks may contain pre-structured information with given constraints, while other tasks may require students to extract information and build the constraints themselves.

Where appropriate, the "problem" or task for students should be clearly stated at the beginning of each item. Each unit should have an introduction clearly stating what kind of tasks students are required to do and what evidence students need to provide.

In any given unit, there should be no more than three source materials to avoid confusion for the students, but generally more than one discipline's information base should be called upon within any unit.

ANALYSES AND REPORTING

One scale will be developed to report the outcomes of the cross-disciplinary problem solving assessment, separate from those being developed for the other major and minor domains of PISA 2003.

The report of the cross-disciplinary assessment of problem solving will be designed to provide policy makers, administrators, teachers, parents and students with a clear picture of students' competencies in problem solving. In particular the reports of results should provide:

- a proficiency scale with accompanying text explaining the nature of students' problem solving capabilities at various points along the scale;

- item maps similar to those used in other OECD/PISA domains to discuss the relative difficulty of item types and to compare student capabilities across items, contexts and other design features;

- data on the relationships existing between students' problem solving performances and performances in other areas of the OECD/PISA assessments;

- special reports that reflect the performance of specific subgroups of students – those of different genders, SES or curricular tracks.

POTENTIAL EXTENSIONS OF THE FRAMEWORK FOR FUTURE OECD/PISA CYCLES

Two options should be considered for future cross-disciplinary problem solving assessments in OECD/PISA. These options involve the assessment of collaborative problem solving, and the use of computer-delivered assessments designed along the lines of the work of Klieme and his colleagues (in press).

Collaborative problem solving

A collaborative problem solving option might consist of a separate block of items students would complete in groups of three. Items in such blocks could be built from items in the regular cross-disciplinary assessment. This would allow for a comparison of students' work in individual settings with their work in collaborative settings. Such assessment blocks would have to allow time for idea generation and formulation and for the development of group roles on the part of the students involved.

The *Pacesetter* programmes of the College Board (2000) have working models of such assessments of collaborative problem solving. Expectations of student competence in problem solving and in education in general require the development of these competencies in an environment that values social or collaborative learning. In that case, they must also be assessed. Given the relation of collaborative problem solving to country-specific goals for students, such an assessment might be developed as an international option within the OECD/ PISA cross-disciplinary problem solving assessment in future cycles.

Computer-based delivery

International interest in students' real-time problem solving capabilities in dynamic settings calls for the development of assessment options that would allow for computer-delivered assessments along the lines described by Klieme (2000). Such assessments provide a rich display of students' problem solving competencies in a dynamic environment. They also allow an examination of how students order and conduct their work in complex settings in a way that no paper-and-pencil based assessment can provide. Such an approach allows for the study of the interaction of pieces of information with the selection of problem solving strategies and the formulation of problem solutions. As with the assessment of collaborative problem solving, the provision of computer-based assessment problems should be considered as an international option in future studies.

ADDITIONAL EXAMPLES

The following units illustrate a range of units, items, and tasks found in the OECD/PISA cross-disciplinary problem solving assessment. These units were used in the field trials for PISA 2003, but not selected for use for one reason or another. However, all deficiencies noted have been repaired, unless otherwise indicated, and these units are offered here as examples of what the units and items in the assessment are like. Since the PISA 2003 assessment was not completed when this publication went to press, no items from that assessment are included here for reasons of test security.

The three units presented here complement the three problem solving units previously presented (Problem Solving Units 1, 2 and 3). These six units provide a fairly complete picture of the variety of problem solving situations in the PISA 2003 problem solving assessment. There are two *decision making* units, two *system analysis and design* units (one on analysis and one on design), and two *trouble shooting* units (one in the context of systems and one using the context of a mechanism). The various items in the units reflect the full range of item formats and response requirements.

The items in the units are presented in boxes with some explanatory comments and notes to illustrate what was expected and what typical student responses were in the field trials. After each unit's items, the marking guide for the unit is presented.

Problem Solving Unit 4
BATTERIES

Problem Solving Unit 4 presents students with a problem context that involves deciding how to determine which brand of batteries is the best to buy to power a personal stereo. Vania has asked four friends to join her in an experiment in which each will try two brands of batteries and then record the length of time each brand powered their individual stereos. The data from Vania and her friends is then provided in tabular form for the students to use in responding to the two items in this unit.

This problem is about deciding which are the best batteries to buy.

Vania notices that some brands of batteries she uses in her personal stereo seem to last longer than others. There are four different brands she can buy that fit her personal stereo. She asks some of her friends to help her decide which is the best brand of battery.

Each of her friends tries two brands of battery in their personal stereos. Figure 1 shows what they tell her. (They use one brand until it runs out and then use another brand until it runs out.) All the batteries have the same voltage rating.

Figure 1 How Long Different Brands of Batteries Lasted

	First brand of battery tried	How long it lasted	Second brand of battery tried	How long it lasted
Vania	N-dure	5 days	Powerpak	5 days
Mark	X-cell	4 days	Hardcell	5 days
Kiki	Powerpak	6 days	Hardcell	5 days
Paul	Hardcell	3 days	N-dure	4 days
Elizabeth	N-dure	7 days	X-cell	4 days

Problem Solving Example 4.1

Vania looks at the results of her investigation and says, "This investigation shows that Powerpak lasts the longest."

Give a reason, based on the results of the investigation, why you could conclude that "Powerpak lasts the longest."

_____

_____

_____

_____

Scoring and comments on Problem Solving Example 4.1

Full Credit

Code 1: • Answers that mention that Powerpak lasts the highest average length of time - $(6+5)/2 = 5.5$. All other battery types have lower averages (N-dure $= 5.33$, X-cell $= 4$, Hardcell $= 4.33$).

> Note: The calculations do not need to be shown for the award of the mark.

OR

• Powerpak lasted 5 days or more. All other types have a lower minimum (4, 4, and 3 days).

No Credit

Code 0: Other answers.

Item type: Open constructed-response
Problem solving type: Decision making
Situation: Personal life / Scientific

This item calls on students to comprehend the nature of testing a product such as batteries and the role that data might play in such a test. Given the data in the table, it appears that some form of comparison of the life of the batteries is a possible response plan. To do so, students are required to recognize that they are being asked to create a comparison and provide some form of justification for their response.

If students approach the item by finding the average battery life and then concluding that Powerpak batteries have the longest life, since their average life is the greatest, then they have examined information, compared alternatives, formed a generalisation, and communicated their results.

Some students failed to grasp what they were asked to do. They interpreted the item as asking for an explanation of the power demands of students' stereos or focused only on the first or second battery tested by the individual students. Some students gave reasons unrelated to the investigation, such as "You can tell from the TV advertisements".

This item may be somewhat similar to an item students may see in consumer economics. For most students, however, this item will be a non-routine item and one that will cause them to think in new ways and form a communication describing their findings.

Problem Solving Example 4.2

Give TWO different reasons why the results of this test may not be reliable.

Scoring and comments on Problem Solving Example 4.2

Possible reasons:

- usage on each day is unspecified in terms of time and purpose (playing, rewinding, volume, etc.);
- the investigation involves a small sample;
- the measurements are crude – what is meant by a "day"?
- the fact that sometimes a battery of the same sort lasts seven days and sometimes four days means that the results are likely to be suspect;
- different stereos may have different power requirements.

Full Credit

Code 2: Answers that mention TWO possible reasons very clearly, from the above list.

> *Note*: the two reasons should be different, and not merely two ways of saying the same thing.

Partial Credit

Code 1: Answers that mention only ONE possible reason very clearly, from the above list.

No Credit

Code 0: Other answers.

Item type: Open constructed-response
Problem solving type: Decision making
Situation: Personal life / Scientific

....

This item calls for students to examine the constraints under which the experiment took place, to note the factors that were possible sources of variation in the life of the batteries, and to examine alternative explanations for the test outcomes.

Some students failed to understand the task and tried to explain why the result noted in Problem Solving Example 4.1 is really true. Other students focused on a particular facet of the situation and gave only one reason, or two equivalent reasons, why the test results may not be reliable. For example, one student's two reasons were that some stereos may have been switched off and on and that the stereos may not have been played for the same amount of time.

Success in responding to this item requires students to have a solid comprehension of the task of testing the life of a battery. This involves being able to list possible factors related to the life of a battery, to examine the interrelationships among these factors, to compare and contrast these factors with those used in responding to Problem Solving Example 4.1 above, and to carefully communicate two alternative explanations that would discredit the response formed by Vania.

The ability to correctly answer this item may be related to students' experience with the scientific method. For this reason, this unit was not included in the main study but saved for use as a sample unit.

Problem Solving Unit 5
ROLLERS

Problem Solving Unit 5 presents students with two problem contexts that deal with analysing how a system of rollers turns and then a context in which they must design a drive belt system that will turn a set of rollers in specified directions.

The introductory material presents a simple roller system and provides figural information about how the rollers in the system rotate, given the direction of the drive roller.

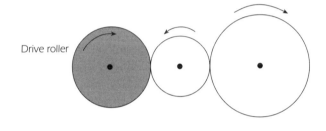

This problem is about designing a set of rollers to turn in a particular way.

A set of rollers can be made to turn by placing the rollers in contact and then turning one of the rollers. The roller turned is called the **drive roller**.

Problem Solving Example 5.1

Here is an arrangement of rollers.

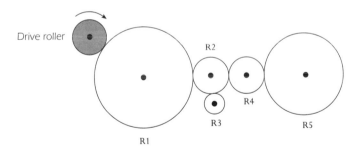

Which roller(s) will turn in the same direction as the drive roller, and which will turn in the opposite direction?

ROLLER	WILL IT TURN IN THE SAME DIRECTION AS THE DRIVE ROLLER OR IN THE OPPOSITE DIRECTION?
R1	Same direction / Opposite direction
R2	Same direction / Opposite direction
R3	Same direction / Opposite direction
R4	Same direction / Opposite direction
R5	Same direction / Opposite direction

Scoring and comments on Problem Solving Example 5.1

Full Credit

Code 1: Answers that specify Opposite, Same, Opposite, Opposite, Same, in that order. (R2 and R5 will turn in the same direction as the drive roller.)

No Credit

Code 0: Any other combination of answers.

Item type: Complex multiple-choice
Problem solving type: System analysis and design
Situation: Personal life / Work and leisure

....

To correctly respond to this item, students must understand the relationship among rollers and how movement takes place in sequential rollers as a result of a movement of the drive roller. Such thought on the part of students calls for them to induce a rule about roller rotation direction based on the example, and perhaps on their understanding of the relationship between successive rollers in similar, familiar settings.

Based on their intuitive understanding of the situation, students then form a generalisation that says, in some form, that successive touching rollers move in opposite directions. This generalisation alone is not sufficient to completely respond to the question asked. Students also have to see this relationship as a transitive relationship: that if A-B-C is a chain of touching rollers, then if A moves clockwise, B moves counter-clockwise, and C again moves clockwise. This transitive understanding allows students to move the explanation through a sequence of successive rollers, perhaps by adding arrows that alternate between clockwise and counter-clockwise from one roller to the next. This understanding is also analogical in nature.

Students' developed abilities to answer the items in this unit are based, in part, on their understanding of mechanical systems and their spatial reasoning. For this reason, this unit was not included in the main study but saved for use as a sample unit.

Problem Solving Example 5.2

Some arrangements of rollers will not turn when the drive roller is turned. Explain why the following arrangement of rollers will not turn.

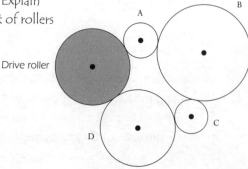

Scoring and comments on Problem Solving Example 5.2

Full Credit

Code 1: Answers that mention that if the drive roller turns clockwise, A will go counter-clockwise, B will go clockwise, C will go counter-clockwise, D will go clockwise, and force the drive roller to go counter-clockwise. Since it is already turning clockwise, movement is not possible.

OR

Answers that mention equivalent statements (check student's markings on the diagram in conjunction with the texts they write.):

- because each roller will be "pushed" in one direction by one roller and in the opposite direction by the other roller with which it is in contact;

- because the drive roller and one of the rollers next to it will be trying to turn in the same direction;

- they will clash, *e.g.*, B and C will want to move in the same direction;

- roller A is turning roller B in a different direction from roller C, so it will not turn.

No Credit

Code 0: Other answers, for example:

- because they are linked, and not in a straight line;
- because they are not joined;
- because they are all going in opposite directions.

Item type: Open constructed-response
Problem solving type: System analysis and design
Situation: Personal life / Work and leisure

....

Like Problem Solving Example 5.1, this item calls on students' comprehension of the relationships among a sequential set of rollers and the ability to transfer this understanding across the many successive sets of rollers in this "ring".

Here students have to put their induced rule concerning the alternating rotation of sequential rollers to the test. This is an act of system analysis. This item calls on students to check specific cases in a particular problem context for consistency with respect to the rule they have formed concerning the rotational behaviour of rollers in a spatially arranged system.

The reasoning in this item is new to many students. Few students have experience in attacking a spatially defined situation and looking for evidence that a particular outcome is not occurring. Analysing a system to find out non-performance is different from most similar school exercises. The "explanations" of many students consisted only of arrows indicating that there was eventually a clash of rotational direction as you moved around the system.

Problem Solving Example 5.3

Another way a set of rollers can be made to turn is by using a drive belt which connects the drive roller to the other rollers. Here are two examples:

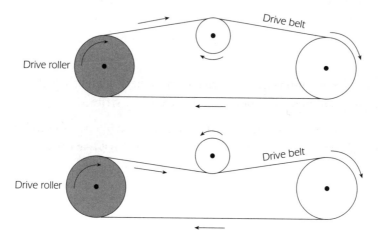

Draw a drive belt around this set of rollers so that all the large rollers turn clockwise and all the small rollers turn anti-clockwise. The belt must not cross over itself.

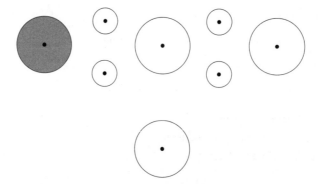

Scoring and comments on Problem Solving Example 5.3

Full Credit

Code 1: Answers that follow the example below.

> *Note* that Code 1 should be awarded even if the belt in the drawing does not actually touch the rollers.

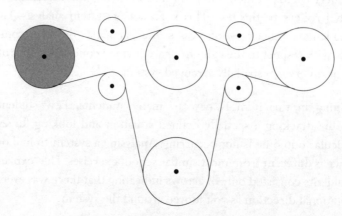

No Credit

Code 0: Other answers.

Item type: Open constructed-response
Problem solving type: System analysis and design
Situation: Personal life / Work and leisure

....

This item involves comprehending the operation of rollers relative to the motion of the drive roller and the contacts between other rollers and the drive belt. In this case, students must induce a rule about the operation of the drive belt and the rotation of the rollers according to whether or not they are on the same side of the drive belt or on opposite sides.

Once students have induced this relationship, they have to check it and then form a design (in this case the placement of the drive belt on the set of rollers provided) and to "build the system" that will carry out the desired rotational effects in the roller set. When students have built their design, they need to check it again to ensure that it creates the desired rotations in the rollers.

This problem has more than one correct solution but "non-symmetric" designs were hardly ever given as student responses.

Problem Solving Unit 6
BOOK SALES

Problem Solving Unit 6 presents students with a problem context that concerns a book company's internet ordering system. The problem involves analysing the book ordering system, trouble shooting where customer address problems might occur, and altering the ordering program to insert a given subprocess that verifies and charges the customer's credit card account.

The unit begins with the presentation of a flow-chart that shows the steps involved in processing a book order placed with the company over the internet.

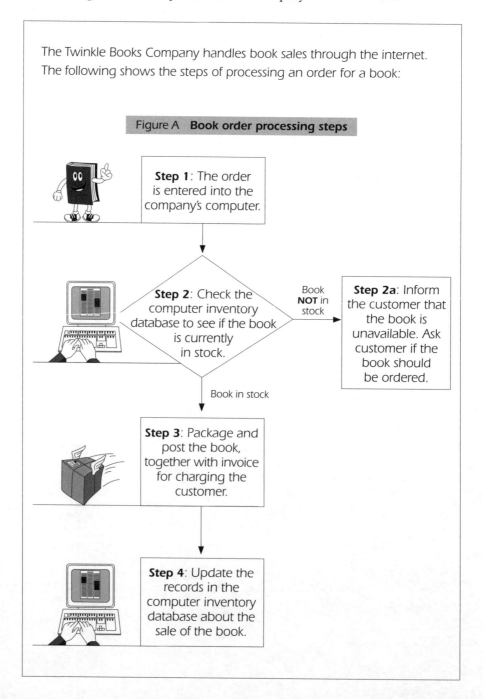

The Twinkle Books Company handles book sales through the internet. The following shows the steps of processing an order for a book:

Figure A   **Book order processing steps**

Step 1: The order is entered into the company's computer.

Step 2: Check the computer inventory database to see if the book is currently in stock.

Book **NOT** in stock

Step 2a: Inform the customer that the book is unavailable. Ask customer if the book should be ordered.

Book in stock

Step 3: Package and post the book, together with invoice for charging the customer.

Step 4: Update the records in the computer inventory database about the sale of the book.

Problem Solving Example 6.1

A book sent to a customer was returned because of an incorrect address. In which step(s) of the process could the error have occurred?

Step	Could the error have occurred in this step?
1	Yes / No
2	Yes / No
2a	Yes / No
3	Yes / No
4	Yes / No

Scoring and comments on Problem Solving Example 6.1

Full Credit

Code 1: Answers that specify Yes, No, No, Yes, No, in that order.

No Credit

Code 0: Any other combination of answers.

Item type: Complex multiple-choice
Problem solving type: Trouble shooting
Situation: Work and leisure

A correct response to Problem Solving Example 6.1 requires students to understand the relationships between the various steps of the procedure, and the directions associated with each one. Understanding such a procedural diagram is crucial to the analysis and trouble shooting of many sequentially designed business procedures, where the temporal aspects of decision making are central to carrying out a procedure such as the present one.

Once students have analysed the procedure, they must diagnose the specific problem presented in the item. In this case, the process involves performing a large number of tests involving conditional reasoning of the form "If this type of error occurs here, then how does it affect the mailing of a package or letter further along in the system?". To correctly carry out the needed trouble shooting steps, the student must be able to reason in settings involving both verbal and diagrammatic information.

Problem Solving Example 6.2

The Twinkle Books Company is having difficulty in getting some customers to pay for their books. As a result, the company wants to require customers to give their credit card number when they order a book.

To do this, the company wants to add the following steps to the process in Figure A.

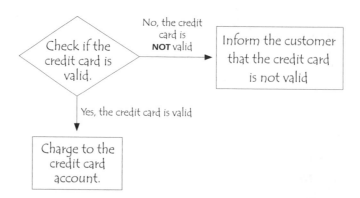

Where in Figure A should you insert the above steps for checking and processing credit card information?

A. Between steps 1 and 2.

B. Between steps 2 and 3.

C. Between steps 2 and 2a.

D. Between steps 3 and 4.

E. After step 4.

Scoring and comments on Problem Solving Example 6.2

Full Credit

Code 1: Response B: Between steps 2 and 3.

> *Note:* The debiting of the charges should not occur until the company is sure that it can deliver the product to the customer.

No Credit

Code 0: Other responses.

Item type: Multiple-choice
Problem solving type: Trouble shooting
Situation: Work and leisure

....

Like Problem Solving Example 6.1, this item requires students to reason from verbal and diagrammatic information to understand sequential aspects of the procedure. However, in addition, in this item the student must design a system by locating, via a careful analysis of the logic involved, where to insert a given subprocess that checks *and charges* a customer's credit card as part of the ordering procedure. Locating the subprocess correctly (*i.e.* between steps 2 and 3) depends on recognising that the customer should not be charged unless the book is in stock.

Many students chose option A (between steps 1 and 2), which may correspond to the practice of some companies. For this reason, and the fact that experience with internet ordering could vary widely among students, this unit was not included in the main study but saved for use as a sample unit. ⌐

REFERENCES

Baxter, G.P. and **R. Glaser** (1997), *An Approach to Analysing the Cognitive Complexity of Science Performance Assessments* (Technical Report 452), National Center for Research on Evaluation, Standards and Student Testing (CRESST), Los Angeles, CA.

Binkley, M.R., **R. Sternberg**, **S. Jones** and **D. Nohara** (1999), *An Overarching Framework for Understanding and Assessing Life Skills,* Unpublished International Life Skills Survey (ILSS) Frameworks, National Center for Education Statistics, Washington, DC.

Bloom, B.S., **J.T. Hasting** and **G.F. Madaus** (1971), *Handbook on Formative and Summative Evaluation of Student Learning,* McGraw-Hill, New York, NY.

Blum, W. (1996), "Anwendungsorientierter Mathematikunterricht – Trends und Perspektiven", in G. Kadunz *et al.* (eds.), *Trends und Perspektiven. Schriftenreihe Didaktik der Mathematik, vol. 23,* Hoelder-Pichler-Tempsky, Wien, Austria, pp. 15-38.

Boshuizen, H.P.A., **C.P.M. van Der Vleuten**, **H.G. Schmidt** and **M. Machiels-Bongaerts** (1997), "Measuring Knowledge and Clinical Reasoning Skills in a Problem-based Curriculum", *Medical Education,* 31, Department of Educational Research and Development University of Limburg, Limburg, Netherlands, pp. 115-121.

Bransford, J.D., **A.L. Brown** and **R.R. Cocking** (eds.) (1999), *How People Learn: Brain, Mind, Experience, and School,* National Academy Press, Washington, DC.

Bybee, R.W. (1997), "Towards an Understanding of Scientific Literacy", in W. Grabe and C. Bolte (eds.), *Scientific Literacy – An International Symposium,* IPN, Kiel, Germany.

Charles, R., **F. Lester** and **P. O'Daffer** (1987), *How to Evaluate Progress in Problem Solving*, National Council of Teachers of Mathematics, Reston, VA.

College Board (2000), See documents on the web at http://www.collegeboard.com/about/association/pace/pacemath.html

Collis, K.F., **T.A. Romberg** and **M.E. Jurdak** (1986), "A Technique for Assessing Mathematical Problem Solving Ability", *Journal for Research in Mathematics Education,* 17(3), pp. 206-221.

Committee of Inquiry into the Teaching of Mathematics in Schools (1982), *Mathematics Counts* (the Cockcroft report), Her Majesty's Stationery Office, London, United Kingdom.

Council of Europe (2001), *Common European Framework of Reference for Languages: Learning, Teaching, Assessment*, Cambridge University Press, Cambridge, United Kingdom.

de Corte, E., **B. Greer** and **L. Verschaffel** (1996) "Mathematics Teaching and Learning", in D. C Berliner and R. C. Calfee (eds.), *Handbook of Educational Psychology,* Macmillan, New York, NY, pp. 491-549.

Csapó, B. (1997), "The Development of Inductive Reasoning: Cross-sectional Assessments in an Educational Context", *International Journal of Behavioral Development,* 20(4), pp. 609-626.

Devlin, K. (1994, 1997), *Mathematics, the Science of Patterns*, Scientific American Library, New York, NY.

Dossey, J. A. (1997), "Defining and Measuring Quantitative Literacy", In L. A. Steen, (ed.), *Why Numbers Count: Quantitative Literacy for Tomorrow's America* (pp.173-186), The College Board, New York, NY.

Dossey, J.A., **I.V.S. Mullis** and **C.Q. Jones** (1993), *Can Our Students Problem Solve?,* National Center for Educational Statistics, Washington, DC.

Einstein, A. (1933), "Preface to M. Plank", *Where is Science Going?,* Allen and Unwin, London, United Kingdom.

Fey, J. (1990), "Quantity", In L. A. Steen (ed.), *On the Shoulders of Giants: New Approaches to Numeracy*, National Academy Press, Washington, DC.

Frensch, P. and **J. Funke** (1995), "Definitions, Traditions, and a General Framework for Understanding Complex Problem Solving", in P. Frensch and J. Funke (eds.), *Complex Problem Solving: The European Perspective,* Lawrence Erlbaum Associates, Hillsdale, NJ, pp. 3-25.

Freudenthal, H. (1973), *Mathematics as an Educational Task*, D. Reidel, Dordrecht, Netherlands.

Freudenthal, H. (1983), *Didactical Phenomenology of Mathematical Structures*, D. Reidel, Dordrecht, Netherlands.

Garfield, J., and **Ahlgren, A.** (1988), "Difficulties in Learning Basic Concepts in Probability and Statistics: Implications for Research", *Journal for Research in Mathematics Education*, 19(1), 44-63.

Gee, J. (1998), *Preamble to a Literacy Program*, Department of Curriculum and Instruction, Madison, WI.

Graeber, W. and **C. Bolte** (eds.) (1997), *Scientific Literacy – An International Symposium,* IPN, Kiel, Germany.

Grünbaum, B. (1985), "Geometry Strikes Again", *Mathematics Magazine*, 58 (1), pp 12-18.

Hawking, S.W. (1988), *A Brief History of Time,* Bantam Press, London, United Kingdom.

Hiebert, J., **T.P. Carpenter**, **E. Fennema**, **L. Fuson**, **P. Human**, **H. Murray**, **A. Olivier** and **D. Wearne** (1996), "Problem Solving as a Basis for Reform in Curriculum and Instruction: The case of Mathematics", *Journal for Research in Mathematics Education,* 25(4), pp. 12-21.

International Labour Office (ILO) (1998), *World Employment Report 1998-1999: Employability in the Global Economy – How Training Matters*, ILO, Geneva, Switzerland.

Kirsch, I.S. and **P.B. Mosenthal** (1989-1991), "Understanding Documents. A Monthly Column", *Journal of Reading,* International Reading Association, Newark, DE.

Klieme, E. (1989), *Mathematisches Problemlösen als Testleistung*, Lang, Frankfurt/Main, Germany.

Klieme, E. (2000), *Assessment of Cross-disciplinary Problem Solving Competencies,* Unpublished paper for Network A, OECD-OECD/PISA, Paris, France.

Klieme, E., **J. Ebach**, **H.J. Didi**, **A. Hensgen**, **K. Heilmann** and **H.K. Meisters** (in press), *Problemlösetest für Sechste und Siebente Klassen*, Hogrefe, Göttingen, Germany.

de Lange, J. (1987), *Mathematics, Insight and Meaning*, OW and OC, Utrecht University, Utrecht, Netherlands.

de Lange, J. (1995), "Assessment: No Change Without Problems", in T.A. Romberg (ed.), *Reform in School Mathematics and Authentic Assessment*, Suny Press, Albany, NY.

de Lange, J. and **H. Verhage** (1992), *Data Visualization,* Sunburst, Pleasantville, NY.

Langer, J. (1995), *Envisioning Literature,* International Reading Association, Newark, DE.

Laugksch, R. C. (2000), "Scientific Literacy: A Conceptual Overview", *Science Education*, 84 (1) 71 –94.

LOGSE (1990), *Ley de Ordenacion General del Sistema Educativo*, Madrid, Spain.

Masters, G., **R. Adams** and **M. Wilson** (1999), "Charting Student Progress", in G. Masters and J. Keeves (eds.), *Advances in Measurement in Educational Research Assessment,* Elsevier Science, Amsterdam, Netherlands.

Masters G. and **M. Forster** (1996), *Progress Maps*, Australian Council for Educational Research, Melbourne, Australia.

Mathematical Association of America (MAA) (1923), *The Reorganization of Mathematics in Secondary Education; A Report of the National Committee on Mathematical Requirements*, The Mathematical Association of America, inc, Oberlin, OH.

Mathematical Sciences Education Board (MSEB) (1990), *Reshaping School Mathematics: A Philosophy and Framework of Curriculum*, National Academy Press, Washington, DC.

Mayer, R.E. (1985), "An Information-processing Analysis of Mathematical Ability", In R.J. Sternberg (ed.), *Human Abilities – An Information-processing Approach*, Freeman, New York, NY.

Mayer, R.E. (1992), *Thinking, Problem Solving, Cognition* (2nd ed.), Freeman, New York, NY.

Mayer, R.E. and **M.C. Wittrock** (1996), "Problem Solving Transfer", in D. C. Berliner and R. C. Clafee (eds.), *Handbook of Educational Psychology*, Macmillan, New York, NY, pp. 45-61.

Mitchell, J., E. Hawkins, P. Jakwerth, F. Stancavage, and **J. Dossey** (2000), *Student Work and Teacher Practice in Mathematics*, National Center for Education Statistics, Washington, DC.

McCurry, D. (2002), *Notes towards an Overarching Model of Cognitive Abilities*, Unpublished report, Australian Council for Educational Research, Melbourne, Australia.

Millar, R. and **J. Osborne** (1998), *Beyond 2000: Science Education for the Future*, King's College London School of Education, London, United Kingdom.

National Council of Teachers of Mathematics (NCTM) (1989), *Curriculum and Evaluation Standards for School Mathematics*, NCTM, Reston, VA.

National Council of Teachers of Mathematics (NCTM) (2000), *Principles and Standards for Mathematics*, NCTM, Reston, VA.

Neubrand, M., R. Biehler, W. Blum, E. Cohors-Fresenborg, L. Flade, N. Knoche, D. Lind, W. Löding, G. Möller and **A. Wynands** (Deutsche OECD/PISA-Expertengruppe Mathematik) (2001), "Grundlagen der Ergänzung des Internationalen OECD/PISA-Mathematik-Tests in der Deutschen Zusatzerhebung", *Zentralblatt für Didaktik der Mathematik 33(2)*, pp. 33 - 45.

Newton, I. (1687), Philosophiae naturalis principia mathematica Auctore Is. Newton, Trin. Coll. Cantab. Soc. Matheseos Professore Lucasiano, & Societatis Regalis Sodali. Imprimatur. S. Pepys, Reg. Soc. Praeses. Julii 5. 1686. Londoni, Jussu Societatis Regiae ac Typis Josephi Streater. Prostat apud plures Bibliopolas. Anno MDDCLXXXVII. (English Translation: *Mathematical Principles of Natural Philosophy*, published by University of California Press, Berkeley, 1934).

Niss, M. (1999), "Kompetencer og Uddannelsesbeskrivelse" (Competencies and subject description), *Uddanneise*, 9, pp. 21-29.

OECD (1999), *Measuring Student Knowledge and Skills – A New Framework for Assessment*, OECD, Paris, France.

OECD (2000), *Measuring Student Knowledge and Skills – The PISA 2000 Assessment of Reading, Mathematical, and Scientific Literacy*, OECD, Paris, France.

OECD (2001a), *Knowledge and Skills for Life – First Results from PISA 2000*, OECD, Paris, France.

OECD (2001b), *The New Economy – Beyond the Hype: The OECD Growth Project*, OECD, Paris, France.

OECD (2002a), *Sample Tasks from the PISA 2000 Assessment: Reading, Mathematical, and Scientific Literacy*, OECD, Paris, France.

OECD (2002b), *Reading for Change – Performance and Engagement across Countries*, OECD, Paris, France.

O'Neil, H. (1999), *A Theoretical Basis for Assessment of Problem Solving*, Unpublished paper presented at the Annual Meeting of the American Education Research Association, University of Southern California, Montreal, Canada.

Polya, G. (1945), *How to Solve It*, Princeton University Press, Princeton, NJ.

Problem Solving Expert Group (PEG) (2001), *Problem Solving and OECD/PISA 2003*, Unpublished paper, OECD/PISA, Paris, France:

Robitaille, D. and **R. Garden** (eds.) (1996), *Research Questions and Study Design*, Pacific Educational Press, Vancouver, Canada.

Romberg, T. (1994), "Classroom Instruction that Fosters Mathematical Thinking and Problem Solving: Connections between Theory and Practice", in A. Schoenfeld (ed.), *Mathematical Thinking and Problem Solving*, Lawrence Erlbaum Associates, Hillsdale, NJ, pp. 287-304.

Ryjchen, D. and **L.H. Salganik** (2000), *Definition and Selection of Key Competencies (DeSeCo)*, OECD, Paris, France.

Schoenfeld, A.H. (1992), "Learning to Think Mathematically: Problem Solving, Metacognition, and Sense-making in Mathematics", in D. A. Grouws (ed.), *Handbook of Research on Mathematics Teaching and Learning*, Macmillan, New York, NY, pp. 334-370.

Schupp, H. (1988), "Anwendungsorientierter Mathematikunterrricht in der Sekundarstufe I Zwischen Tradition und Neuen Impulsen" (Application-oriented mathematics lessons in the lower secondary between tradition and new impulses), *Der Mathematikunterricht*, 34(6), pp. 5-16.

Seger, M.S.R. (1997), "An Alternative for Assessing Problem Solving Skills: The Overall Test", *Studies in Educational Evaluation*, 23(4), pp. 373-398.

Shamos, M.H. (1995), *The Myth of Scientific Literacy*, Rutgers University Press, New Brunswick, NJ.

Steen, L.A. (1990), *On the Shoulders of Giants: New Approaches to Numeracy*, National Academy Press, Washington, DC.

Steen, L. A. (ed.) (1997), *Why Numbers Count: Quantitative Literacy for Tomorrow's America*, The College Board, New York, N.Y.

Stern, D. (1999), "Improving Pathways in the United States from High School to College and Career", *Preparing Youth for the 21st Century – The Transition from Education to the Labour Market*, OECD, Paris, France.

Stewart, K. (1990), "Change", In L. A. Steen (ed.), *On the Shoulders of Giants: New Approaches to Numeracy*, National Academy Press, Washington, DC.

Sticht, T.G. (ed.) (1975), *Reading for Working: A Functional Literacy Anthology*, Human Resources Research Organization, Alexandria, VA.

Stiggins, R.J. (1982), "An Analysis of the Dimensions of Job-related Reading", *Reading World, 82*, pp. 237-247.

Swaak, J. and **T. de Jong** (1996), "Measuring Intuitive Knowledge in Science: The Development of the What-if Test", *Studies in Educational Evaluation*, 22(4), pp. 341-362.

Trier, U. and **J. Peschar** (1995), "Cross-Curricular Competencies: Rational and Strategy for Developing a New Indicator", *Measuring What Students Learn*, OECD, Paris, France, pp. 99-109.

Tversky, A., and **D. Kahneman** (1974), "Judgements under Uncertainty: Heuristics and Biases", *Science*, 185, pp. 1124-1131.

UNESCO (1993*), International Forum on Scientific and Technological Literacy for All*, Final Report, UNESCO, Paris, France.

U.S. Department of Labor (1991), *The Secretary's Commission on Achieving Necessary Skills (SCANS): What Work Requires of Schools*, U.S. Department of Labor, Washington, DC.

Vosniadou, S. and **A. Ortony** (1989), *Similarity and Analogical Reasoning*, Cambridge University Press, New York, NY.

Ziman, J. M. (1980), *Teaching and Learning about Science and Society*, Cambridge University Press, Cambridge, United Kingdom. ⌡

PISA 2003 Expert Groups

Mathematics Expert Group (MEG)

Jan de Lange, Chair
Utrecht University
Utrecht, Netherlands

Werner Blum, Deputy Chair
University of Kassel
Kassel, Germany

Mary Lindquist, Deputy Chair
Columbus, GA, United States

Vladimír Burjan
EXAM
Slovak Republic

Sean Close
St Patricks College
Dublin, Ireland

John Dossey
Illinois State University
Normal, IL, United States

Zbigniew Marciniak
Warsaw University
Warsaw, Poland

Mogens Niss
IMFUFA, Roskilde University
Roskilde, Denmark

Kyungmee Park
Hongik University
Seoul, Korea

Luis Rico
Universidad de Granada
Granada, Spain

Yoshinori Shimizu
Tokyo Gakugei University
Tokyo, Japan

Reading Expert Group (REG)

Irwin Kirsch, Chair
Educational Testing Service
Princeton, NJ, United States

Marilyn Binkley
National Center for Educational Statistics
Washington, DC, United States

Alan Davies
University of Edinburgh
Scotland, United Kingdom

Stan Jones
Statistics Canada
Nova Scotia, Canada

John H.A.L. de Jong
Language Testing Services
Velp, Netherlands

Dominique Lafontaine
Université de Liège
Liège, Belgium

Pirjo Linnakylä
University of Jyväskylä
Jyväskylä, Finland

Martine Rémond
Institut National de Recherche Pédagogique
Paris, France

Science Expert Group (SEG)	Problem Solving Expert Group (PSEG)
Wynne Harlen, Chair University of Bristol United Kingdom	John Dossey, Chair Illinois State University Normal, IL, United States
Peter Fensham Monash University Melbourne, Australia	Benő Csapó University of Szeged Szeged, Hungary
Raul Gagliardi Geneva, Switzerland	Wynne Harlen Berwickshire, United Kingdom
Svein Lie University of Oslo Oslo, Norway	Ton de Jong University of Twente Twente, Netherlands
Manfred Prenzel Leibniz-Institute for Science Education at the University of Kiel Kiel, Germany	Irwin Kirsch Educational Testing Service Princeton, NJ, United States
Senta A. Raizen National Center for Improving Science Education Washington, DC, United States	Eckhard Klieme German Institute for International Educational Research Frankfurt/Main, Germany
Donghee Shin Dankook University Seoul, Korea	Jan de Lange Utrecht University Utrecht, Netherlands
Elizabeth Stage University of California Oakland, CA, United States	Stella Vosniadou University of Athens Athens, Greece

OECD PUBLICATIONS, 2, rue André-Pascal, 75775 PARIS CEDEX 16
PRINTED IN FRANCE
(96 2003 05 1 P) ISBN 92-64-10172-1 – No. 53161 2003